Praise for *State of War*

"In *State of War*, his gripping, electrifying study of the brutal Salvadoran gang culture, William Wheeler dramatizes with almost painful immediacy a vital truth: that all the fevered talk about a "crisis at the border" is really an ignorant lament about what three decades of U.S. foreign policy have wrought. At its core, the so-called crisis is about what we as Americans have done to El Salvador and its Central American neighbors. To confront the savage violence ripping through those countries and sending their citizens on a desperate flight north is ultimately to find oneself gazing at the American face in the mirror. With his vivid prose and intrepid reporting, Wheeler has shown us the bloody consequences borne by real people— and given us a powerful, unforgettable book."

—Mark Danner,
author of *The Massacre at El Mozote*
and *Spiral: Trapped in the Forever War*

"Brisk, chilling examination of El Salvador's descent into violence and the role of notorious transnational gang MS-13. Journalist Wheeler combines a clear sense of geopolitical history and gutsy on-the-ground reporting, producing a compact tale of a slow-motion, violent societal collapse."

—*Kirkus Reviews*

State of War
MS-13 and El Salvador's World of Violence

COLUMBIA GLOBAL REPORTS
NEW YORK

State of War

MS-13 and
El Salvador's
World of Violence

William Wheeler

Los Angeles

United States

Mexico

State of War
MS-13 and El Salvador's World of Violence
Copyright © 2020 by William Wheeler
All rights reserved

Published by Columbia Global Reports
91 Claremont Avenue, Suite 515
New York, NY 10027
globalreports.columbia.edu
facebook.com/columbiaglobalreports
@columbiaGR

Library of Congress Control Number: 2019952210
ISBN: 978-1-7336237-2-8
E-book ISBN: 978-1-7336237-3-5

Book design by Strick&Williams
Map design by Jeffrey L. Ward
Author photograph by Miranda Sita

Printed in the United States of America

For my family

CONTENTS

October 15, 1979—The Revolutionary Government Junta overthrows the right-wing military regime of President Gen. Carlos Humberto Romero in a coup. The U.S. administration of Jimmy Carter fears the country will fall to a leftist, communist uprising, and throws its support behind the new military government with millions of dollars in arms and spending. The junta violently represses civilians and the leftist guerrilla group Farabundo Martí National Liberation Front (FMLN), and many Salvadorans flee to the U.S. for safety.

March 24, 1980—Archbishop of San Salvador Óscar Romero calls on the military and death squads to refuse government orders to kill civilians, and is assassinated during Mass. A quarter of a million people attend his funeral a week later as government-ordered snipers shoot and kill forty-two mourners. The outrage and the following insurrection of the FMLN mark the start of the Salvadoran Civil War.

MS-13 is founded in Los Angeles in the same year.

December 11, 1981—A Salvadoran army unit, the Atlacatl Battalion, founded, equipped, trained, and directed by U.S. military advisers in El Salvador, kills as many as one thousand unarmed civilians accused of collaborating with the FMLN in the infamous El Mozote Massacre. The Reagan administration backs the junta by denying the massacre, calling it leftist propaganda spread by the FMLN.

1982—The Nationalist Republican Alliance (ARENA), an extreme right-wing party, wins parliamentary elections marked by violence. The civil war and government massacres of civilians continue. U.S. officers take on leadership positions in the Salvadoran military to run the war. The Reagan administration increases military aid to El Salvador to $2 million a day.

1984—Christian Democrat José Napoleón Duarte wins the presidency against the ARENA's Army Major Roberto D'Aubuisson, becoming the first Salvadoran civilian president since 1931. Military continues its

14   war against the FMLN. Army massacres and attacks by death squads
      organized by D'Aubuisson continue.

      1989—ARENA candidate Alfredo Cristiani voted president in elections
      widely believed to have been rigged; FMLN attacks intensify in an
      offensive aimed at toppling Cristiani.

      1991—Bush administration approves $42.5 million in military aid to
      El Salvador's government. Death squad killings continue. Peace talks
      between ARENA and FMLN begin.

      January 16, 1992—The ARENA government and the FMLN sign
      UN-sponsored Chapultepec Peace Accords, ending the civil war. Over
      12 years, more than 80,000 people were killed, half a million fled El
      Salvador as refugees, and half a million more were internally displaced.
      The FMLN is recognized as a political party.

      1996—Bill Clinton signs into law the Illegal Immigration Reform and
      Immigrant Responsibility Act of 1996, resulting in the deportation of
      many MS-13 gang members to El Salvador. MS-13 and Barrio 18 become
      more powerful in El Salvador and the Northern Triangle.

      2003—President Francisco Flores Pérez launches "iron fist" measures to
      combat the gangs, calling it Plan Mano Dura, reviving his ARENA party's
      political prospects.

      2004—ARENA candidate Antonio Saca wins presidential elections in
      March. In August, he launches Plan Super Mano Dura. In September,
      following deadly clashes in overcrowded prisons, he accedes to gang
      demands and assigns the Ciudad Barrios and Quezaltepeque prisons
      to MS-13 and the Chalatenango and Cojutepeque prisons to Barrio 18,
      which become de facto headquarters of the gangs' leadership.

      2009—El Salvador becomes the most homicidal country in the world,
      with a rate of 71 murders per 100,000 people. In March, for the first time
      since the war, ARENA loses the presidency, as FMLN candidate Mauricio
      Funes wins presidential elections.

2010 June—A faction of Barrio 18 sets fire to a bus full of civilians, killing seventeen people. President Funes returns to Mano Dura—style laws backed by advertising campaigns.

September—A few days after the Salvadoran Congress approves a new anti-gang law, MS-13 and Barrio 18 demand a public transport strike. The government responds by sending two thousand soldiers to the streets.

2011 September—U.S. adds El Salvador to list of countries considered major producers or transit routes for illegal drugs.

2012 March—*El Faro* breaks the story that the government has secretly negotiated a truce between MS-13 and Barrio 18 factions after transferring their leaders to minimum security prisons.

2013—Murder rate in El Salvador drops to 39.4 per 100,000 inhabitants.

2014—FMLN congressman Benito Lara approaches gang leaders to reopen talks in order to help party win the elections by mobilizing new voters and intimidating the opposition. ARENA learns about the secret negotiations and holds its own secret meeting with the gangs. Gang members decide to stick with the FMLN. In March, FMLN's Salvador Sánchez Cerén scores narrow win in presidential election.

June—Cerén takes office as the first former rebel to become president and cuts off all support for the truce. Lara is named security minister. The U.S. speeds up deportations to cope with the growing number of migrants from Central America. El Salvador, Honduras, and Guatemala receive millions of dollars to combat gang violence and help those deported from the U.S.

2015—Cerén sends gang leadership back to maximum-security prison and announces his own tougher version of Plan Mano Dura.

2016—With the murder rate at 104 homicides per 100,000 people, Cerén announces a set of "extraordinary measures," a return to "iron fist" policies, to combat the gangs.

State of War
MS-13 and
El Salvador's
World of Violence

Introduction

Israel Ticas is racing down the highway, drumming his hands on the wheel of "The Beast," a tall, boxy police service truck that he aims at the small, bustling town of San Luis Talpa, about twenty-five miles south of El Salvador's capital, San Salvador. A decades-long veteran of the security forces, Ticas's first job was as an artist in the counter-terrorism unit, sketching suspected guerillas during the country's 1979–1992 civil war. "I was the last person these guys would see before the person who killed them," he tells me, flatly. The experience left him equally as distrustful of the right-wing generals he had served as of the guerilla commanders who would join them among the political elite at war's end. In most ways, the country has never quite recovered since. In 2015, homicides in El Salvador rivaled the most violent peak of the civil war, and it ranks consistently among the world's most violent nations. Before long, Ticas spots a body by the roadside. "It's fresh," he observes. "With clothes on." It hasn't been stripped or dismembered. The victim, he says, was likely shot at that spot during the night.

Ticas calls himself a "lawyer for the dead." A self-taught forensic criminologist, he locates and digs up the bodies of victims of gang killings, and in so doing, he documents the crimes of the country's notorious *maras*. On this hot March morning in 2018, his finger is wrapped thick with gauze—a few days earlier, he pricked it on a thorn covered in fluids from decomposing cadavers. His belt is adorned with a skull and crossbones pattern. As always, he carries a pistol in a handbag at his side.

But we aren't here for the body by the roadside. Instead, we stop outside a two-story concrete building where men in blue-and-white camouflage uniforms armed with assault rifles are milling about. Our security detail piles into a Toyota Hilux, and we follow them zigzagging out of town and into the surrounding sugarcane fields, the convoy kicking up a bright cloud of swirling dust. Our destination is a site used by members of the local MS-13 clique to rape, torture, and execute people. The victims include civilians, rivals from the Barrio 18 gang, and their own members who break internal codes of discipline. After a few minutes, the convoy stops at a parched basin beside the fields, a spot where a river runs during the wetter months.

As the river rises and falls in the jungle terrain, Ticas explains, the land swells and crumbles. So the topography has all changed since the site was in use, several years ago, and his informant has struggled to remember where all the bodies are buried. Still, Ticas has managed to find eleven of the twenty-one remains his informant says are buried here. The attorney general gave Ticas three months to work the location, and today is the deadline. He thinks he can find one more before his time is up, and he's brought the informant here to help.

20 Ticas's informant is a lanky young man who wears a bala-clava to hide his face. The night of the murder was his initiation, when he got a call and was summoned to the site. When he arrived, he was told to dig a hole: A woman would be killed. The woman and her partner had recently moved to town, and the clique suspected the couple had problems with MS-13 elsewhere. After an "investigation," the gang "disappeared" her partner. Grief-stricken, the woman confronted members of the clique, screaming at them in the street, threatening to tell the police. The clique decided to kill her as well. A civilian was instructed to get the woman drunk in her home, just up the road from the burial site. Then she would be brought to the informant. His job, the informant was told, would be to cut her head off—"to prove you have balls." But one of the gang members rushed the job and struck her in the back of the head with a machete. She wandered the house in a stupor, like a zombie, smearing her blood on the walls. So he struck her again. And again. And again.

Ticas asks him if the victim died in her house or whether they finished her off at the burial ground. "She was in agony," the informant says, but not dead. They removed her clothes and dragged her here, then began to chop her up.

Ticas and his team shovel out the topsoil until they reach hard-packed earth, then sweep away the dust with brooms. He surveys the crust, looking for a patch of discolored soil, a sign that something has been altered. With his fingers he traces the boundaries of what he sees in the dirt. His men dig down a layer around its perimeter, then level the ground flat. He draws the outline again and they dig a layer deeper. Gradually, an oval silhouette appears, the result of soil that has been dug up, oxygenated, and repacked. Ticas works the site laterally, instructing his men to dig a trench beside the cavity. They sift the dirt they extract through a sieve, looking for any clues the perpetrators or the victim might have left behind.

Ticas moves around the grave in a dizzying pattern, fishing out roots and rocks, working his way around the hole like a pool shark. The cavity has roughly the shape of the African continent. In the lower right corner, about where Tanzania might be, is a fist-sized hole. He reaches elbow-deep into it, and feels what he knows by touch to be a human pelvic bone. It most likely belonged to a woman, the hole having been formed by the decomposition of the fleshy mass around her hips. Over several hours, he combs away the dirt, exposing a human skeleton. Its head is bent backward, as if in supplication.

"It's weird," says the informant. He was sure they had buried her deeper. The limbs seem largely intact, with bits of tattered clothing around them. Ticas clears away dirt from the skull. He uses a turkey baster to clean the scalp, then fishes out broken shards from its face. "Talk to me," he mutters to the bones. "What do you want to tell me?" After reconstructing her neck, vertebrae by vertebrae, Ticas gathers her ribs into a pile by the spine. He notes the slash marks on her breastbone.

Something else is amiss. The informant's victim would have suffered machete wounds to the back of the head, but this cranium is intact. Instead, the front of the skull shows signs of being hacked repeatedly. Ticas concludes, in the end, that it belongs to a different woman altogether—a name that was not on the informant's list. It's the third body they have found here that the informant knew nothing about.

"We haven't even found a quarter of the fucked-up things these assholes have done," says a member of the police detail keeping watch over Ticas and his crew. He, too, wears a mask, with an assault rifle slung over his shoulder, in case the gang's spotters are watching. Of late the gang has been disappearing off-duty members of the police and military and their families.

The murders that occurred here happened in the middle of a truce that the government negotiated between the rival gangs, which was credited with cutting the homicide rate in half. But the reality, the informant says, is that it taught them to hide their victims in clandestine graves like these. Ticas was not formally trained in forensics, and many of the techniques he uses he discovered himself. But he's not the only one learning in the process. First, he noticed that the gangs had begun dismembering corpses so they would fit into smaller holes, making them tougher to spot. Later, they began stabbing the corpses in the stomach and throat before burying them in order to release gases trapped inside, so the decomposition process would leave an even smaller cavity. As they worked to cover up their crimes with increasing sophistication, they even joked that they were making it a challenge for Ticas, the informant tells him.

The informant had lived in the United States for a decade when, in 2013, he was suddenly deported after missing a court appointment, he says. As soon as he arrived at his family's house in El Salvador, members of MS-13 showed up at his doorstep. Everyone here must collaborate, they told him. He started as a lookout, but before long they said he knew too much about them and would have to join the gang. Today, at twenty-four, he has already committed thirty-one murders, he claims. His manner is earnest and agreeable. But Ticas tells me the informant would just as soon murder us all. "We have a working relationship," Ticas says. "But he's a psychopath."

A few months ago, the informant fell out of favor with his clique. His first offense was "unauthorized drinking"— members have to ask for permission before consuming alcohol, since intoxication renders them unreliable. Then shortly after, he survived a police ambush. The gang assumed he was a collaborator, and they tried to kill him, though he survived again. So he went to the police and said he could give them information on twenty murders. So far, 105 arrests have been made because of his cooperation.

In addition to revealing where the bodies are buried, the informant must name names and testify against his former clique. Unlike in the U.S., where he would presumably be offered witness protection, in El Salvador he lives on his own, even while the gang would like nothing more than to find and kill him, which they will likely succeed in doing if he doesn't leave the country when the case is finished.

Ticas tells me that he also expects to one day be killed by the gangs. In one scene in *The Engineer*, a documentary about Ticas, a gang member says that if they ever catch him off guard, they'll bury him in one of the very graves he has been excavating.

But for now, today was a good day. Ticas even thinks he knows the identity of the victim they've found. At the start of this case, the daughter of a missing woman came to him asking for his help. "Have faith," he told her. "God will help me find your mother." Each corpse that goes undiscovered is another family that will never get closure. "It's days like this that I know that God does miracles," he says.

———

In his first State of the Union address, President Donald Trump railed against "the savage gang MS-13," and called on Congress "to finally close the deadly loopholes that have allowed MS-13, and other criminals, to break into our country." The gang is the president's favorite public menace to invoke in his bid to convince Americans that illegal immigration constitutes an urgent crisis and a threat to national security (second only, perhaps, to an "invasion" of migrants in caravans seeking asylum in the U.S.—a great many of whom, ironically, are trying to flee the gang's reach).

Rather than a problem to be deported away, however, the reality of the gang is considerably more complex. Born out of the ecology of Los Angeles's fierce gang warfare, MS-13 was founded in the 1980s by Salvadoran refugees who had been hardened in a brutal civil war still raging at home. In time, the gang expanded to include other nationalities, and it spread to other American cities. Today, in the United States, it numbers no more than ten thousand members and functions mostly—their penchant for sensational violence aside—like an average American street gang, fighting to control neighborhood turf and local drug sales.

In the late 1990s, the Latino gangs of Los Angeles found an export mechanism: In response to MS-13's growing clout and amid Bill Clinton's own immigration crackdown, the U.S. began deporting foreign-born residents convicted of wide-ranging crimes. Thousands of convicts were sent back to the Northern Triangle each year—the neighboring Central American countries of El Salvador, Honduras, and Guatemala. Among them were members of MS-13 and their L.A. rivals, the Eighteenth Street gang, or Barrio 18. In the Hobbesian landscape of a region

reeling from endemic poverty, wars, and political violence, the
struggle for survival and dominance of these Americanized
gangsters produced a sociological phenomenon.

El Salvador had small, disorganized neighborhood gangs
before the war. But, according to a popular view in El Salvador,
these mass deportations changed everything in the country.
Many have come to believe that the U.S. got rid of their problem
at El Salvador's expense. The state's institutions had been
gutted by conflict, poverty, and corruption. The deportees came
back from the streets of Los Angeles with tattoos and baggy
clothes, and brought along with them gang culture, urban warfare tactics, and criminal networks from prison. The Salvadoran
youths, a generation of jobless foot soldiers who made easy
recruits, flocked to their banner. The *maras*, as the gangs are
known, have since drawn three generations into an escalating
cycle of conflict that offers no easy escape. Today the countries
of the Northern Triangle, where the *maras* predominate, rank
among the world's highest murder rates, and account for 75 percent of the migrants arriving at the U.S.'s southern border. The
maras, in this analysis, are the primary and most urgent problem
facing countries like El Salvador.

El Salvador's government and its law enforcement have been
quick to support this view. According to Salvadoran government numbers, there are sixty thousand gang members—and
some ten percent of the population dependent on or otherwise
tied to the gangs—in a country of just over six million.

It's not difficult to understand why the authorities are eager
to depict El Salvador's violence as the original sin. Doing so has
allowed the Salvadoran regime to blame the cause not only on
a gang culture imported from America, but on often simplified

26   notions of crime that have little to do with difficult and costly political solutions. Making the gangs the focus of the country's troubles allows the government to put off engaging with more urgent and deep-seated problems such as corruption, lack of state institutions, and inequality. Thus, politicians have introduced violent and repressive "iron fist" measures to much fanfare, often prior to key elections, suggesting that such hardline programs are populist means to attract voter support, even though evidence suggests that the gangs' power has only grown as a result. The *maras*, so goes the conventional wisdom, are a crime problem, best countered with severe police and even military force.

The conclusion that I reached was more complicated than what the Salvadoran authorities like to portray. The country's violence was not only the result of American-imported crime. It was always determined by the legacy of El Salvador's civil war and the underlying inequality that had precipitated it but was nonetheless never resolved by its outcome. For both of these factors, the U.S. indeed bore considerable responsibility. But neither would be remedied alone by police killing of *mareros* or the mass imprisonment of gang members. If anything, American assistance to Salvadoran regimes to help tackle root problems that had been exacerbated by the war and its aftermath were in order. Successive Salvadoran governments, with American support, have done little, if anything, to address these issues, and have more often made these problems worse.

The *maras* will not simply be killed off or arrested away. Neither will the consequences of their continuing evolution be walled off behind national boundaries, increasingly intertwined as they are with the currents of illicit supply and demand that tie producers to the U.S., the world's largest market for illegal drugs. As U.S.-led interdiction efforts in Mexico, Colombia, and the Caribbean have pushed trafficking routes into Central America—now the transit corridor for an estimated 88 percent of U.S.-bound cocaine—the *maras* have come into closer contact with trafficking organizations like the Sinaloa cartel and the Zetas, for whom they work as contractors and hired guns.

Meanwhile, behind the noisy spectacle of the "Muslim ban" and family separations and the deployment of the U.S. military to its southern border, the Trump administration has quietly enacted a wide range of calibrated policy changes to dramatically ramp up the deportation machinery it inherited, and to choke off immigration across the board. To name just two: the removal of domestic violence or persecution by gangs—conjoined crises in the region—as grounds for asylum in the U.S.; and the end of Temporary Protected Status that has allowed hundreds of thousands of Central Americans to remain in the U.S. legally for years. El Salvador is one of the countries that's most dependent on remittances from abroad, and the fate of some 200,000 of its citizens now hangs before U.S. courts as they decide whether Trump has the authority to revoke their legal status. The human toll of all these changes will be devastating. Of those affected, many will remain in the U.S., working under the table and living in the shadows. Others will be forced back to the countries of their birth and meet violent ends. Many more will return, both clients and cargo of the human smuggling networks now controlled by organized crime. If history is a guide, the gangs will only emerge stronger as a result.

The story of El Salvador's gang problem, I learned in the course of reporting, is a study in shortsighted thinking—from

28 governments in both Washington and San Salvador, on both sides of the political spectrum—that has backfired, at best, in the form of unintended consequences or, more cynically, traded political points for a failing strategy driving the country to ruin. In every direction, I found evidence of a war that never really ended.

One final note: In many places throughout the book, I refer to a source by a pseudonym because identifying him by name would put his life at risk: in the case of former gang members, because they had turned informant or because, as a retired female member of Barrio 18 told me, they were still considered soldiers and would be held responsible for their words; in the case of former cops, because they would be targeted by gang members, including those who had infiltrated their ranks, or even the officials who had been their superiors.

"A Large Scale Exodus"

Alex Sanchez was seven years old in 1979, when he crossed the southern border of the United States along with his younger brother under the care of a *coyote,* a people-smuggler. The start of the civil war back home wouldn't come until the following year, when a gunman would assassinate Archbishop Óscar Romero, an outspoken critic of his government's ongoing campaign of torture and repression, as he gave Mass in a church-run hospital in San Salvador. But the violence had been building for years. Several times, while on his way to school, Sanchez had passed the gruesome spectacle of a corpse dismembered by machete, which the army had left on display in the street as a sort of public warning. His parents had gone ahead a few years earlier to settle in Los Angeles. Now, at last, they had sent for him. Arriving in California—against the backdrop of Disneyland and the iconic Hollywood hills that Sanchez knew from news broadcasts—it was possible to believe in all the promise of a new beginning.

30   Gradually, the contours of their new reality came into focus. The family was crammed into a one-bedroom apartment in the neighborhood around MacArthur Park, a run-down section of central L.A. that had been abandoned a decade earlier in the flight to the suburbs. His parents were undocumented, working under the table. Sanchez felt the burden he represented as another mouth to feed, even as he bristled at the parental authority he had learned to live without. He spoke no English, and quickly learned that Salvadorans were viewed with disdain in the predominately Mexican community. Sanchez's mother dealt with the pressures in her own way, becoming a Jehovah's Witness. She took Alex with her as she went from door to door in their neighborhood to proselytize, and to congregation, where he would give occasional sermons. Among his classmates, however, this only reinforced his isolation. Frequently bullied, he found himself alone at the bottom of an unforgiving food chain.

Soon enough, Sanchez would find allies among the waves of Central Americans fleeing class-based struggles and the dismal economies that had produced them. Back in El Salvador, a quarter-million people turned out for Archbishop Romero's funeral in 1980, when shadowy forces suddenly attacked the crowd, detonating explosives and shooting down at people from rooftops and windows.

The country quickly descended into a vicious civil war, which pitted a coalition of leftist guerilla groups against a right-wing government backed by Washington. Right-wing leader Roberto D'Aubuisson admitted, according to a declassified 1982 State Department memo, that the death squads stalking the population were in fact comprised of official security forces whose "members use the guise of the death squad

when a potentially embarrassing or odious task needs to be per-
formed." Members of an infamous U.S.-created battalion would
go on to massacre entire villages.

This was the Cold War, and the threat of another communist victory in its backyard was something that Washington
wanted to avoid. So the United States sent military advisers and
materiel, spending more than $4.5 billion to prop up the Sal-
vadoran regime over the course of a war that dragged on for
twelve years and claimed 75,000 lives before ending in a stale-
mate. Throughout, most Salvadorans found themselves caught
in the middle, as Joan Didion observed, "in a country where the
left had no interest in keeping peasants less 'radicalized' and
the right remained unconvinced that these peasants could not
simply be eliminated."

Not surprisingly, roughly a million of them left, half of
whom sought safety and a better life in the U.S. They settled
mostly in Los Angeles, flooding into the neighborhood around
MacArthur Park, where their outsider status was compounded
by their legal reality as undocumented immigrants. Adhering to
the standard set by the context of the Second World War, the
U.S. limits its definition of a refugee to someone persecuted
because of race, religion, nationality, political opinion, or social
group. Those merely seeking a haven from generalized violence don't qualify. Political expediency has always played a role
in U.S. refugee policy, though, and exceptions were made for
those fleeing Washington's Cold War enemies, including communist regimes in Vietnam, the Soviet Union, Cuba, and Nic-
aragua. But to have made a similar exception for those fleeing
Washington's ally would be to admit an uncomfortable reality
of America's foreign policy. Churches and Central American

32   immigrant groups joined forces to advocate for Salvadorans and
        Guatemalans (the latter involved in a devastating civil war that
        would claim 200,000 lives), filing a 1985 lawsuit that eventu-
        ally secured them work permits and the opportunity to reapply
        for asylum.

        Nonetheless, their presence contributed to a growing anti-
        immigrant sentiment. The following year, Ronald Reagan signed
        into law the Immigration Reform and Control Act, which tried
        to disincentivize illegal immigration by tightening control of
        the border and slapping business owners who hired undocu-
        mented labor with stricter penalties—the first major revision
        of immigration law in decades. Apparently the move scared Sal-
        vadoran president José Napoleón Duarte, who was worried that
        a flood of returning Salvadorans would destabilize a govern-
        ment teetering on the brink of defeat. Reagan wrote to reassure
        him, acknowledging "that the sudden return of many thousands
        of Salvadorans now in the U.S. could, as you point out, have a
        disastrous effect on El Salvador." Reagan had been assured that
        "a large scale exodus of undocumented Salvadorans" from the
        U.S. was not expected as a result of the policy, he continued, and
        promised that Duarte's concerns would be relayed to the proper
        officials in order to keep the undocumented Salvadorans right
        where they were.

        Where they were, in Sanchez's case, was forming the van-
        guard of MS-13. Rather than a Salvadoran import, they were, like
        the gangs of New York before them, the by-product of a particu-
        larly American urban experience. "In a pattern that has become
        familiar," writes Al Valdez, a retired police officer and gang
        expert, "the predatory and dynamic Los Angeles street environ-
        ment in which immigrant Salvadorian youth found themselves

became the catalyst that compelled the first Mara Salvatrucha cliques to form."

By this time, Sanchez had found protection and solidarity in a circle of pot-smoking Salvadoran metalheads. They came from families like his that had been split up in the process of emigrating, then reassembled with stepparents and new siblings. They were unwanted—in both the country that had displaced them and the country where they landed—and angry about it. When they rebelled, their parents resorted to extreme discipline to straighten them out. They called themselves the "Mara Salvatrucha Stoners."

When Sanchez was jumped in, his initiation consisted of a vicious beating by the other members for a period of thirteen seconds (thirteen being the Gothic number for bad luck). At fourteen, he ran away from home and gave himself the nickname "El Rebelde," The Rebel. Sanchez and his friends were sleeping on rooftops and in abandoned houses. But for the first time he felt free.

L.A.'s first Latino gangs had sprung up, a century earlier, in the barrios where Mexican families who had been living in the area for generations began falling back in the face of what today might be called gentrification. Bound by culture and the shared experience of marginalization in the wider, whiter society, they were largely protective of their communities. By the late 1960s, Mexican youth, facing harassment from local gangs whose membership was limited to U.S. citizens of pure Hispanic heritage, had banded together in Sanchez's neighborhood to form Barrio 18—a group that would become Sanchez's rivals and the city's second-most notorious international export.

In the diverse tapestry of L.A.'s gang life, the Mara Salvatrucha Stoners emerged from among dozens of so-called

34 "stoner gangs" roaming the city since the mid-1970s. "Mara,"
which derives from the name from a particularly ferocious
ant, refers to one's circle of friends. "Salva" comes from Salvadoran. "Trucha" means "trout" but connotes something like
"beware." Together, the name might loosely translate to "watch
out for my Salvadoran crew." They dressed in tight, roughed-up
bell-bottoms, grew their hair long down their backs, and wore
Converse shoes, whose five-pointed star logo resembled the
pentagram. Unlike the Chicano gangs, these Salvadoran stoners
were more likely to be dropping acid in the mosh pit than out
looking for fights. They took as their hand signal heavy met-
al's devil horn salute—a fist with the index and little finger
extended—which members today flash on the streets and tag on
the walls of slums across Central America.

Their rise and early predilection for the macabre was also
animated by ghosts of war in the combat experience of a small
core of veterans from the conflict back in El Salvador. Among
the 150 or so early members who anthropologist T. W. Ward
interviewed for his book *Gangsters Without Borders: An Ethnography of a Salvadoran Street Gang*, six had fought with the guerillas and seven with the Salvadoran military (including some
who had been trained in counterinsurgency tactics at the infamous U.S.-run School of the Americas). Their numbers also
included a handful of animal-sacrificing Satanists, only adding
to their street cred. The gang cultivated the mythology: A reputation as human-sacrificing devil-worshippers proved handy in
Los Angeles.

Sanchez and his friends began stealing cars, at a time when
an arrest record became a badge of honor. As they circulated
through juvenile hall, they began to mirror the style and attitude

of the Chicano gangs they mixed with in order to fit in. They cut their long hair and slicked it back under hairnets, traded their bell-bottoms for baggy khakis and their Converse for Nike Cortez with knee-high socks. On the outside, as they moved in bigger numbers, they drew the attention of the city's dominant Latino and African American gangs and those gangs began to target them. Before long, two of Sanchez's associates had been murdered by rivals to show their dominance, drawing them all deeper into the ecology of conflict.

The gang learned early on the power of fear, as Sanchez recognized the first time he saw an MS-13 member whip out a machete during a massive rumble in MacArthur Park. Salvadorans were used to machetes as an agricultural tool. But the sight of the blade elicited a level of shock in their rivals that left an impression—it reminded him of the corpses in the streets of San Salvador. Soon the machete became their signature weapon. A cycle of escalation followed. The machetes became guns. Guns became Uzis. Soon the weapon of choice was the AK-47. Eventually, Sanchez would come to see gangbanging as something close to suicide. A rival gang member was just another version of himself; it was like looking in the mirror and wanting to destroy what he saw.

By this time, Valdez writes, the laws governing the barrios were being rewritten. Even as the new ethnic groups streaming into the city were absorbed into the existing order or fighting to establish their own, the established Mexican street gangs "had come to believe that the turf they claimed was theirs by right, no matter what changes had come to the Barrio." Local residents and shop owners became prey as the gangs consolidated and extended their reach over whole communities through

36   force and intimidation. "There were no rules except that only
      the strong survived and that the more you were feared, the more
      respect, control, and power your gang would have." Increasingly,
      the clearest route to power was lined with drugs.

      African American street gangs like the Bloods and the Crips,
      which had emerged during the 1960s, controlled the crack trade.
      But the Latino gangs were the fastest growing and constituted
      the majority of gang members in Los Angeles County. Control of
      the local drug market, meanwhile, was monetizing turf, giving
      each group a reason to fight for every park, stoop, and street
      corner like they owned it. Between 1988 and 1991, gang mem-
      bership in Los Angeles County, now the gang capital of America,
      doubled from 50,000 members in 450 gangs to 100,000 in 750
      gangs. Still, something like an uneasy peace existed between
      the city's different ethnic gangs, with the majority of violence
      occurring within each group, not between them.

      But then Los Angeles exploded—in the form of the L.A.
      riots. The irony was not lost on Sanchez that public fear over the
      threat posed by the city's African American and Latino gangs
      quickly overshadowed concern about the legacy of police bru-
      tality and racial animus that had triggered the violence, on dis-
      play in the videotaped beating of Rodney King at the hands of
      LAPD officers. One of its consequences, however, was an escala-
      tion of "black and brown" violence and a resulting push for con-
      solidation and control of the Latino gangs by the Mexican Mafia.
      "La Eme" had originated in the 1960s, taking control of the con-
      traband trade in California prisons. But this prison gang had
      since grown into an organized and highly disciplined force. From
      behind the walls of maximum-security facilities like Northern

California's Pelican Bay prison, La Eme set itself up as a distributor between Mexican cartels and the Southern California Latino street gangs they used as muscle, particularly Barrio 18. In 1992, La Eme demanded these gangs pay a "tax" on all their drug profits, which would ostensibly go to a fund to help incarcerated gang members. Most obeyed. Others, including some MS cliques, refused. In response, La Eme put them on a "green light list" that allowed others to kill them at will. These cliques flaunted their independence with tattoos that proclaimed them to be "green lighters" or "tax free."

In the wake of mounting death tolls between the Latino gangs, a Mexican Mafia leader sent out an edict to stop the violence, which eventually culminated in a truce between the Latino gangs. While the media portrayed this as a public-spirited gesture, gang defectors later described it as a means by which La Eme inserted an agent to enforce its tax collection from the gangs and extend its control over the region's drug trade. In the process, this prison gang backed by its "Sureño" gang structure became Southern California's most powerful organized crime syndicate. Valdez, the former cop, acknowledges that the net effect was "to impose at least a degree of discipline at the street level . . . if only because drugged up operatives and misdirected violence attract the attention of authorities and cut into profits." But Sanchez saw it as something more. Tapped to negotiate peace with La Eme, he became an emissary to the restive factions that had resisted its yoke. He was summoned to a meeting—in a park, no weapons—of the city's Latino gang leaders, who were eager to exchange phone numbers and bring him into the fold to help establish boundaries and adjudicate

38   disputes. They were part of a system, Sanchez learned, which
had the power not only to collect taxes and administer territory
but also to regulate violence, waging war or bringing peace to
the streets. In hindsight, he would come to believe that this was
what had so frightened authorities.

But a strong state brooks no such challenge. Law enforcement soon hit back with racketeering charges and court-ordered
injunctions that banned gang members from appearing together
in public. In response to Mara Salvatrucha's growing clout, Sanchez watched authorities increasingly target them, and many of
his associates fanned out to start franchises in smaller towns
across the state. Amid the police abuses that followed, Valdez
would conclude the injunctions had failed because most came
without funds to improve life in the communities that had fostered the gangs or any way out for those who wanted one. The
lure of new markets, meanwhile, was driving the gangs' expansion across the country, as L.A.'s gang problem was quickly
becoming America's. Salvadoran hubs in Washington, D.C., and
New York City were magnets. The concept of turf was changing
as the gang migrated, from the strictly defined territory of the
barrio to basically anywhere a clique found itself. In Los Angeles
County, gang-related deaths would peak at 807 in 1995, nearly
double the rate from seven years earlier, and total gang membership would reach 150,000 people in 1,100 gangs.

One of Sanchez's protégés from that time, who went by the
street name Angel de la Muerte (Angel of Death), was part of
that migration. When we met, in a jail in El Salvador, he cited
another reason for his departure from Los Angeles: Alex Sanchez. Angel remembered him in the highest terms—as "a

natural born killer." Sanchez was eloquent and had a conscience. He looked out for the younger guys. But when he had the devil in him, he was to be avoided at all costs. Angel wanted to be like Sanchez when he grew up—which was one of the reasons his family moved him away from California.

Angel had been born in San Miguel, El Salvador, in 1975. His memories of the country are also punctuated with scenes of people being murdered by machete. A decade later, his family left for the U.S. after his father, a member of Salvadoran special forces, was killed by a grenade blast. Three years later, when he was thirteen, Angel walked across the desert with a *coyote* to join them in Los Angeles. He was told it was the good life there. When he arrived, his grandmother told him to focus on school. But his new Salvadoran friends told him to follow their lead. Angel took to drinking and smoking, wearing bandannas and baggy jeans sagging low on his hips. They told him he was one of them now and could have any girl he liked. He told himself he had found the good life. One afternoon, he was sitting with a girl he liked on a stoop, surrounded by his friends, when a car rolled past spraying bullets, killing her. His friends told him they knew who was responsible. They asked if he wanted revenge, if he wanted to get his letters. It was like the devil whispering in his ear. That night he became a trigger-puller. The next day, they jumped him in. He felt proud. The first time he pulled the trigger, he liked it. The devil gets into you when you commit your first murder, he believed. He was thirteen years old. They joked that one day he would be their leader.

In 1995, Angel's family moved him to Virginia, a move that coincided with the expansion of Latino gangs across the country. In Virginia, Angel soon fell back into the good life. He liked the

40   fast money and the cocaine. He became the leader of a clique, and things quickly went off the rails. It wasn't like the early days, when they would provide for their homies in jail. Before long he was traveling Mexico linking up with drug kingpins and murdering his friends for money. One night, in 1998, SWAT busted down his door and caught him with nearly a kilo of cocaine. By that time Latino gangs had established themselves in forty-eight states, including small towns across the heartland.

In California, Sanchez was caught in the revolving door between prison and the barrio, where LAPD anti-gang units were now working hand in hand with immigration agents. Voters had passed the state's "Three Strikes" measure mandating a life sentence for repeat offenders of serious crimes, and Governor Pete Wilson had ridden to reelection on a ballot that curbed undocumented immigrants' access to healthcare, education, and welfare. It was an austere new era in which "Latino immigrant youth, alongside African Americans, became fodder for the flourishing prison industrial complex, fed as it was by the war on drugs playing out on the streets of inner-city neighborhoods," as University of California professor Elana Zilberg writes. "This growing relationship between criminal and immigration law culminated in 1996 with the passage of the Illegal Immigration Reform and Immigrant Responsibility Act of 1996, which mandated the deportation of immigrants—documented or undocumented—with criminal records at the end of their jail sentences."

Sanchez had suspected the end of El Salvador's civil war, in 1992, would clear the obstacles to deporting Salvadorans. But still a boundary remained between immigration and law

enforcement. Only repeat offenders already known to
immigration—those without any documentation at all—would
ever get deported. Green card holders were never deported.
Whenever one of his friends was arrested, the judge would usu-
ally just funnel him into the proper channels to normalize his
immigration status.

But the political winds were shifting. In 1994, Republi-
cans took control of the U.S. Congress in midterm elections,
many of whom had seized on immigration as a central campaign
issue. As part of a post-midterm pivot, President Bill Clinton
signed into law tough crime and welfare bills followed by the
1996 Illegal Immigration Reform and Immigrant Responsibility Act. With a stroke of the pen, Clinton "invented immigration enforcement as we know it today," as journalist Dara Lind
put it, laying the legal framework for the massive deportation
machinery with which his successors would later be associated.
Prior to the law, immigration enforcement within the country's
interior had been minimal. The new immigration policies the
bill enacted, however, scaled up the number of people who were
deportable while scaling down those who could qualify for legal
status. The net effect would dramatically increase the number
of people living illegally in the U.S. In the decade following the
bill, the number of people living in the U.S. illegally grew from
5 million to 12 million, including at least 5.3 million people—
or roughly half the undocumented population today—who
would have qualified for legal status if it were not for the bill's
new restrictions, according to estimates by sociologist Douglas
Massey. A few months after it was passed, Clinton adviser Rahm
Emmanuel argued that a tough stance on immigration could be

42   a winning strategy, outlining how an aggressive effort to "claim and achieve record deportations of criminal aliens" would allow the administration to do with immigration what it had with crime.

Now, shoplifting had become enough to trigger an automatic deportation—an export mechanism that would ultimately help spread Sanchez's gang across the western hemisphere. Judges were talking about "a new mandate," and police were out looking for gang members and handing them over to immigration authorities right away, regardless of whether they had a green card or a work permit. Immigrant community leaders were silent on the issue, obsessed with promoting the "model immigrant" image with which they still hoped to rally support for comprehensive reform despite the shifting political winds (as they had earlier been silent on California's "Three Strikes" measure, considering it an issue for the African American community). No one was going to speak up on behalf of the gang-banger, who had already wasted his chance at a new life. As a result, Sanchez's homies were getting deported left and right. In the process, Mara Salvatrucha and Barrio 18 would go on to establish themselves not only across the Northern Triangle countries of Guatemala, El Salvador, and Honduras, but also to European cities, primarily in Spain and Italy.

Finally, it was Sanchez's turn. He had no desire to leave the country, having become a father a month earlier. But neither did he see the wisdom of remaining in detention while fighting a case he knew he would lose. So he signed his deportation order and got ready to start over with a clean slate. Sanchez had learned English and thought he could find work in El

Salvador's tourism industry. He would have no criminal record
there. For the first time he wouldn't have to worry about immigration officials or the LAPD. Besides, he was looking forward to seeing the lakes and the beaches and all the places his friends in Los Angeles had told him about.

Then he found himself at the airport in San Salvador, holding a piece of paper with an address written on it. Sanchez had been told to find a taxi and that if he acted like he knew where he was going he would get there. En route, he spotted a large boulder alongside the highway that was tagged with his gang's initials. That made sense, he thought—a lot of his friends had been deported. But it was a reality check that the past was not far behind him. Farther down the road, he caught sight of a wall stenciled with Roman numerals: XVIII. It was the tag of his enemies in Barrio 18. His guard sprang up. It was a familiar survival instinct, a state of hypervigilance that had him scanning his environment for threats. He felt like he was back in prison. Or the streets of Los Angeles.

In the neighborhood where he settled, he was confronted by a new reality: He was a tattooed gang member in a country he barely knew, a country that didn't want him. His new neighbors were talking. Almost immediately, a group of young men confronted him, threatening to kill him. They were MS-13, they told him, and they believed him to be from Barrio 18. Sanchez called his L.A. contacts and got connected to deported gang members in El Salvador who could vouch for him. The kids who were threatening to kill him turned out to have no connections to MS-13 at all; they had started the clique on their own. When he challenged them, they backed down, and asked him to jump them in. That morning they were willing to kill him. Now they

44   wanted him to beat them up and initiate them into his gang. He found it surreal. The guys in his new neighborhood could have just as easily encountered one of his rivals from Barrio 18 and joined up with them. Better to have them protecting him, Sanchez told himself.

This was happening all across the country. Sanchez saw how many others were being deported, then falling back on their survival skills as a gang member. Authorities had not been tipped off they were coming, and nothing like a database of criminal deportees existed. The larger society shunned them, all except for the kids in the slums. He would find them begging at the bus stop, sniffing glue out of paper bags. To these kids who had been abandoned by the left and the right, the gangs gave a mythos and a mantra: "Live for the barrio, die for the barrio." Their neighbors used to spit at them, but now the neighborhood would be theirs. Of the first members he initiated, one had fought with the guerillas, and another with the army. They had their own stockpile of grenades.

One of the first recruits in what became the MS stronghold of Arce, Manuel joined the gang in 1989, when he was eleven years old. The war was entering its tenth and bloodiest year. It was what he had grown up with: waiting for his father to come home late because the guerillas were torching buses on the road; hiding under the bed while a battle raged in the local cemetery; listening while his aunts harangued his mother to get her children out of El Salvador. His family had left in waves, while Manuel remained behind with his mother. Their neighborhood had already fed its share of sons to the conflict, including soldiers like Ernesto "Smokey" Miranda who fled to Los Angeles

and became founding members of MS-13. Manuel had been   45
introduced to the gang by his cousin, whose parents had sent
him back to El Salvador for a spell to get away from trouble in
Los Angeles. Striding through the neighborhood under the wing
of this tall, tattooed gangster, he felt strong. The older kids who
had bullied him looked at him differently. A few months later,
Manuel found a few deported gang members to jump him in. He
told himself he didn't need to fear the gunfire anymore. Now he
could shoot back. He jumped in two friends. They talked about
how this was going to be something big, something that would
leave a mark. Years later, he would see Mara Salvatrucha as a
monster he helped create, a cancer he spread. But at the time
he wanted to be the bravest gangster. The most tattooed. The
evilest criminal. All of it.

Like the young foot soldiers Sanchez and the other deported
gang members were recruiting to their banner, Manuel was
part of a new generation of *mareros* that would soon surpass
their predecessors in sophistication and brutality. At the time,
joining a gang was neither a way to make a living nor yet a fate
one was born into along with his neighborhood. What Manuel
and the rest were selling was family. There was a young home-
less kid in the neighborhood who they called "Little Devil." His
mother worked as a prostitute, and he would go around bare-
foot in ragged clothes. At first, they offered him food. When
they decided to recruit him, they warned him of the dangers.
But Little Devil replied that he had nothing to lose. They told
him that he was not alone anymore and that they would love and
protect him. One day, an older boy beat him up in the park. They
gave the Little Devil a knife and returned en masse to confront
him. Manuel and the others proclaimed that Little Devil was

46   part of the *mara* now. Then the young boy stabbed his attacker in
front of his new brothers. Food, protection, belonging. In a poor
and shell-shocked country where one-fifth of the population
had been driven out, this proved a powerful combination.

Their circles expanded rapidly, especially after the 1992
peace accord was signed—which put an end to the war and,
presumably, the need for a haven from it in the United States.
The U.S. began sending gang members back by the planeload.
Manuel would get a call from an MS member in a California
prison telling him the name of a homie who was about to be
deported and where to find him. Then Manuel would go meet
him and help establish his clique. He discovered a formula. Soon
Manuel was traveling widely, throwing parties to identify recent
deportees, then setting up each as the leader of a new clique. It
became a franchise.

The boundaries of membership were still fluid then.
Deported members from a gang like the Barrio 18, whose rivalry
with MS had carried over to Central America, might try to settle
in their neighborhood, and in those early days would not be
murdered outright. Some they chased away. Others were even
allowed to stay as long as they became *calmado*, a status approx-
imating retired. There were still ways out, short of death, for
their own members then, too. One, who went by the name "El
Mafioso," brought his mother to beg his friends to let him leave
the gang. They snickered, but conceded.

Their crime was still anything but organized. The *mara* was
just a neighborhood crew, the guys on the corner their neighbors would cross the street to avoid. Having not yet discovered extortion, each was left to his own hustle and responsible
for contributing $10 or $20 each week to the gang's coffers. But

the country was awash with guns and men who had learned to use them. Throughout the 1990s, former soldiers and guerillas alike joined the small bands of delinquents that specialized in crime, like forgery or car theft, which proliferated after demobilization. Around 1998, according to Manuel, a colonel who saw by Manuel's tattoos and powerlifter-build that he was a *marero* approached him with a job offer. The colonel was a partner in a series of check-cashing centers, he said, and was forming an assault unit to rob them. He took Manuel to a local police academy for firearms training and introduced him to a few of the officers who would be part of his team. During his first robbery, Manuel wore a police uniform they loaned him for the job. Manuel's claim of military and law enforcement involvement in organized crime might seem like a sensational accusation to level at state institutions, but there is evidence from all over the world to suggest that, in fact, the two go hand in hand. The lack of resolution to a civil war and the inability of a weak state to absorb and reintegrate rebels and militants is just the type of situation that fosters a cooperative and codependent military and criminal regime. According to Manuel and many *mara* and military sources I spoke to, over the 1990s, MS-13 thrived not despite, but because of, the state.

The Iron Fist

In the decade of international stewardship following the end of the civil war, El Salvador was frequently covered as a success story, of sorts. The country's two warring factions—the left-wing FMLN and the right-wing ARENA—evolved into established political parties, contending fiercely but peaceably for power. Civil society organizations flowered along with human rights reforms. The U.S. set to work building up a new civilian police force, the PNC, which had been a key sticking point in the negotiations that produced the peace accord. This force was de-linked from military and intelligence functions, no longer allowed to use torture for forced confessions or extrajudicial killing as modus operandi. Legal reforms followed that established protections for juvenile offenders and assurances of due process.

This anti-hardline, human rights—oriented approach, which dominated Salvadoran law enforcement from 1992 to 2003, was never without its critics. In El Salvador, the dynamic between security and human rights is often viewed as a competitive

one. According to a 1998 poll from the Jesuit-run University
of Central America, 45 percent of the country backed "social
cleansing" of those responsible for the mounting crime rates.
By that time, the ghosts of the civil war had reemerged in the
form of death squads, like La Sombra Negra (The Black Shadow),
this time targeting gang members instead of guerillas.

So how much can the U.S. be blamed for the onset of Latin
America's gang crisis? It's a fraught question, especially since
Salvadoran authorities and gang members alike have an incen-
tive to point the finger elsewhere, promoting a narrative that
muckraking journalists can too easily accept. A recent analysis
from the International Crisis Group tried to answer the question
by comparing murder rates in Salvadoran areas of high and low
gang presence against the number of Salvadorans with a criminal
record deported each year, from 1995 to 2010. (The first MS-13
and Barrio 18 deportees began to arrive in El Salvador as early as
1989, but it wasn't until Clinton-era policies came into effect in
the mid-1990s that the era of "mass deportations" began.)

Plotted on a graph, the three sets of numbers do seem to
track with each other closely for the first seven years. It was
during this time that Sanchez's generation—tattooed and
muscle-bound from prison with freshly creased Dickies and
Nike Cortez, the detritus of their brush with the American
dream—landed as big fish in El Salvador's pond. They recruited
"a generation of adolescents and teens for whom the Cold War
had no relevance and the future held no promise," as Salvadoran
journalist Carlos Martinez writes, and "put down deep roots
among those already marginalized by society."

On the graph, the trend lines rise together like a ramp so
that by the year 2000: annual criminal deportations roughly

50   double to around 2,000 people; the murder rate in areas with
low gang presence doubles to roughly 30 per 100,000 people;
and in high-gang-presence areas it doubles to around 50 murders per 100,000 people (a murder rate ten times as high as that
in the U.S.).

Over the next two years, they all decline slightly. Then,
in 2003, they diverge. The trend line of the murders in low-
gang-presence areas stays relatively flat, meandering like a goat
path through the foothills. Meanwhile, as the impacts of the
U.S. Homeland Security Act begin to take effect and unprecedented levels of funding are channeled to U.S. immigration
enforcement, deportations begin to rise to heights not seen
since the Great Depression. Annual criminal deportations
chart a steep ascent, doubling by 2006, then doubling again by
2010 to more than 8,000 people per year. In areas of high gang
presence, the effect seems to pull the trend line upward along
a parallel path of cascading peaks, doubling again by 2006 to
more than 70 murders per 100,000 people. "This strong correlation between U.S. deportations and homicide rates in the
receiving country suggests some sort of causal link between
the two," the report concludes. "Although U.S. policies sought
to curb criminal activity by breaking up Los Angeles gangs, the
long-term effect was an increase in violence across Central
America and particularly El Salvador."

Perhaps. The number of actual gang members deported was
relatively small, according to Al Valdez, numbering some 5,000
in the first critical years. Immigrants don't engage in crime
any more than the general population, his work has shown—
"the immigrant community was scapegoated because of the
actions of a few." The effect of the deportations was like putting

a bacterial culture in a petri dish. "It's germ food, the perfect environment," he said. "When we started changing our deportation laws, we were taking little germs and putting them in a petri dish in the countries we call Mexico and the Northern Triangle countries. And conditions were ripe for these gangs to grow. And that's exactly what happened."

But the numbers tell another story as well, one that coincides with the spike in the murder rate and constitutes the first of the gangs' two major transformations: the divergence between life in the poor, marginalized communities where most deportees settle and the gangs commit the vast majority of their killing, and the middle- and upper-class communities who live in relative safety yet continue to support an exclusively military and mass-incarceration response. This approach was modeled after zero-tolerance policing in American cities, encouraged by U.S. law enforcement agencies, and funded with American aid.

The resurgence of the repressive approach came, in 2003, in the form of President Francisco Flores's Plan Mano Dura (Plan of the Firm Hand, or iron fist). His ARENA party had just suffered its first major defeat at the polls, giving up a majority in the legislature for the first time since the civil war, and presidential elections were looming the following year. "All the world blamed Francisco Flores," said Carlos Martinez, whose online newspaper, *El Faro*, has done some of the most consistent work on the gang beat in Latin America. As a result, Flores needed to shift the discourse from his government's lack of investment in social programs and the fact he had "put millionaire businessmen at the head of a political party that pretends to govern a poor country," Martinez said. "And the response that he found,

52   which in practice was very intelligent, was converting the gangs
      that up until then had been a marginal problem into the enemy.
      The common enemy. The perfect enemy. The perfect evil."

      He was helped by the emergence of a cell-phone video that
      depicted a brutal murder by U.S. criminal deportees—the first
      in a series of gruesome mutilations and decapitations attributed
      to Barrio 18. A public campaign followed that spotlighted gangs
      as public enemy number one. Then one night in June, Flores
      faced the television cameras, wearing a black leather jacket and
      standing in front of a wall tagged with Barrio 18 graffiti, and
      announced a sweep of mass arrests, calling for tough new laws
      to combat the gang menace.

      The rollout of Plan Mano Dura came accompanied with
      telegenic scenes of soldiers and helicopters. "It made him look
      like a very strong president," said Martinez. It gave police prob-
      able cause to arrest suspected gang members, who were swept
      up for petty infractions and funneled into the justice system.
      Supporting legislation increased prison sentences for minors
      and outlawed tattoos and gang membership, along with a host
      of other activities. According to UCSD professor Elana Zil-
      berg, this reflects the "transnationalization" of zero-tolerance
      gang abatement strategies most senior police officers had
      already been exposed to in U.S. embassy–sponsored visits to
      police departments in Los Angeles, Houston, Boston, Chicago,
      and New York. (Former New York City mayor Rudolph Giuliani
      would go on to champion these strategies as a highly paid secu-
      rity consultant across Latin America.) "Mano Dura and the anti-
      gang laws draw upon U.S. legislation such as the Street Ter-
      rorism Enforcement Prevention Act (STEP) and anti-loitering
      laws, which were designed to retake command of the politically

marked space of the street and to prohibit or make 'illicit' all
forms of association and communication between two or more
presumed 'gang members'—be they standing, sitting, walking,
driving, gathering, appearing, whistling, or gesturing—anywhere in public view, which is to say, *in* the streets of the *barrio*."

In legal terms, this had three effects. "To ban gangs. To ban
being a gang member. And it also allowed police to arrest people
for their appearance," said Martinez. "The gangs already had to
deal with similar laws in California." So they adapted. In reality,
the plan was "a big bluff." But while the provisions of Plan Mano
Dura were struck down by the Supreme Court on constitutional
grounds, the plan was a great political success. When Flores's
successor, Antonio Saca, took office the next year, he introduced
a slightly tweaked version of the plan. "It's a publicity exercise
that isn't very creative. His plan was called Super Mano Dura,"
said Martinez. "These two presidents lost years they could have
spent trying to understand the phenomenon, understand why
it generated roots so deep, so quickly. Who were they? Why did
they fight? What is their socioeconomic profile? Their educa-
tional profile? Their family profile? They didn't ask any of this.
Because when someone is bad, there is nothing interesting to
know about bad. Except that it belongs in prison for as long
as possible. While these politicians pursued an electoral and
publicity-oriented strategy to the phenomenon, the gangs went
on mutating and evolving."

Rodrigo Avila, a member of Congress and former Director
General of the PNC who took part in the plan's conception,
surprised me by agreeing with Martinez. "Mano Dura was not
a plan," he said, struggling to find the words to define what it
really was. "It was just PR. Not even PR. It was, like, 'a plan' in

54   quotes." We talked in a hotel restaurant near San Salvador's diplomatic quarter. Despite being stricken by a ghastly cold, Avila
was enlivened by antipathy on the subject. "It was tailored to
create a public perception of the government being hard on
gangs," he said. "That's it. There was no plan. It never existed."

Studies have shown that Salvadoran voters will tip toward
one or the other of the two largest parties depending on whether
they are most immediately concerned with the economy or
with crime. At the time, ARENA was bleeding votes in the face
of Central America's lowest economic growth rate when polling
revealed that nearly half the population had come to view security as their overriding concern. A leaked memo from ARE-
NA's executive committee around this time revealed the shift
in calculus, as populist support for Mano Dura gave the party
a chance to capitalize on voters' fears. On the campaign trail,
Saca promised to get even tougher on the gangs. "So everybody
applauded," said Avila.

The relief was short-lived. The police would round up suspected gang members only to see them released within days
for lack of evidence. During the first year of the plan, 19,275
gang-related detentions were recorded, and 95 percent of the
cases were dismissed. For the gang members it became a badge
of honor, said Avila. "Sometimes they would come and throw
rocks at the police just to get arrested because they knew that
in no time they were going to be released again anyway." Over
the first year of Mano Dura, the murder rate actually rose, from
2,172 murders to 2,762, an increase of more than a murder a day.

But Mano Dura had more lasting effects. According to
Sonja Wolf, these transformations were the "unintended but,

in some ways, inevitable consequences of a deeply flawed ideo-
logical plan." Both MS-13 and Barrio 18 raised the bar to entry,
requiring riskier initiation rites. They also restricted drug use
and became more disciplined. In response to new changes that
made it easier for prosecutors to offer informants leniency,
aspiring gang members now had to kill to join. Avila describes
a proliferation of corpses turning up with fifty rounds in them
or hacked into bloody bits, as prospective gang members took
turns shooting their victims or passing around a machete so
that all would be implicated equally.

Prison officials and police units were ill-resourced to contain the surging violence in the streets or in the country's jails.
In September 2004, the same week that Saca announced "Super
Mano Dura," prison officials quietly implemented a policy that
would radically alter the course of the country's violence: They
gave the gangs their own prisons. For years the deplorable conditions in El Salvador's overcrowded jails had been a visible
symptom of neglect, a symbol of the official lack of capacity or
commitment to contain the surging bloodshed. El Salvador's
penitentiary system had been built to hold 8,000 inmates but
by 2004 was straining with a population of 12,000 (a number
that would triple to 36,000 over the next twelve years). On the
heels of an August 2004 riot that killed thirty-two prisoners in
La Esperanza, authorities who were desperate to maintain some
measure of control finally conceded to one of Mara Salvatrucha's demands. On September 2, they transferred more than a
thousand inmates between four prisons, each of which would
become the exclusive domain of one of the two warring gangs.
Chaletenango prison became the headquarters of Barrio 18,

56   while Mara Salvatrucha set up shop in Ciudad Barrios prison. Both were less like a hermetically sealed penitentiary system than "a market where everything is bought and sold," as Martinez wrote of Ciudad Barrios, where "the prisoners shut themselves in the cells at night because they wish to, as a courtesy to the system."

Thrown together into such an environment and handed the keys, each gang developed a pecking order that allowed them to govern with a new coherence. Mara Salvatrucha, having learned from the Mexican Mafia how to rule the streets from behind prison walls, created a leadership called the *ranfla* that still rules today. The obedience they commanded from their new headquarters was based on the inevitability of a prison stint in the life of a Salvadoran gangster. "All gang members assume that sooner or later they will serve time in prison, and once inside it is better to be surrounded by friends than enemies," as Martinez wrote. "Moreover, if a gang member disobeys a *ranfla* and is later arrested, he knows that in El Salvador he will not be sent to just any prison, but one controlled by the very gang leadership he crossed. And he will pay for his transgression." These gang-run prisons became the site of nonstop meetings in which the new crop of leaders could communicate orders—via visitors and cell phones—to a network that now reached across the entire country. In the case of Barrio 18, a brutal new leader, Viejo Lin, murdered the rivals who opposed his centralization of power, splitting the gang in two. With a national leadership came national policies and financial strategies, most notably extortion. But extortion required killing to enforce it. And the killing begat more killing—a cycle in which the country remains trapped.

Killing came easily enough for Cesar the first time—to say otherwise would be a lie. He had grown up in a family of five that seemed no different from most of the other families on the block. His father worked the graveyard shift as a car lot security guard, splitting his time between two families, while his mother washed clothes in other people's homes. They both worked hard to provide what they could. But something was missing, and Cesar went looking for it in the streets. Where he lived, there wasn't much to do—the lone, trash-strewn soccer field was unusable. He wanted to be part of something. In his neighborhood, the only thing he could think to be a part of was a gang.

The neighborhood then was still dominated by the Mara Salvatrucha thugs who would abuse Cesar on his way to school, smacking him in the head and taking his money. By his early teens, however, a clique from Barrio 18 had expanded to the borders of the neighborhood and was looking for recruits to help eliminate their rivals. In 2002, when gang members approached him about collaborating as a lookout, a *poste,* Cesar agreed. For the next couple years, his main job was to spot any MS members who were drunk or alone, with their guard down. Then he would tip off the shot-caller, the *palabrero,* who would send someone to kill them. Along the way, the gang drew him in closer. The appeal was undeniable. The *palabrero* had money. He had women. He had drugs. He smoked and drank and no one told him what to do. The other *veteranos* groomed Cesar as well, telling him they were going to be his brothers, his family. They would look out for him.

When Cesar was seventeen, he and the other lookouts were offered the chance to become full-fledged *mareros*. No one had to think twice. In the last few years, they had helped kill nearly twenty MS members; refusing the offer would make one a liability. But that never even entered into Cesar's calculation. He wanted in, whatever the price. A few years earlier, the only cost of initiation was the swarm of fists he'd endure in the ritual eighteen-second beatdown. But times were changing. The firm hand of the state was around everyone's throat. Too many were turning informant, and those without blood on their hands were always the first to talk. Now everyone first had to kill to join the gang.

The *palabrero* gave Cesar a gun, named the MS member that he should kill and the time to strike. Then he dispatched him to their enemy's territory. When the hour came, Cesar spotted his target loitering on the corner, and paused to study him from a distance. He had known the young man casually across the divide of the neighborhood's shifting boundaries. But Cesar's own gang affiliation was still a secret. He scanned the faces on the street, worried he might be recognized, and watched for any passing police patrols. When the street was clear, he approached his victim and greeted him warmly. The young man was waiting for his girlfriend, he said. Cesar nodded, chatting him up for a brief moment. Then, in a flash, he pulled out the pistol. The other boy bolted, trying to run. But Cesar was at nearly point-blank range, and squeezed off a round that caught the boy in the head. Then, for good measure, he emptied the revolver into his victim's body on the pavement.

Cesar fled, making his way quickly through the startled streets. Once home, he took a shower. Killing was easy, he realized. When the moment came, he had acted on instinct and adrenaline. Nothing more. Afterward, he felt no guilt or sense of any unseen boundary crossed. He felt nothing. So Cesar changed his clothes and returned to the crime scene, blending into the crowd milling around the body. Another gang member would later tell him that, in Los Angeles, the police had such training and technical resources that they nearly always got to the bottom of a murder. Here, an hour after his first kill, the police hadn't even arrived to take note of the corpse.

As soon as Cesar was jumped in, he realized he'd been lied to. The gang was supposed to be a tribe of equals. But once he became a homeboy, the façade of egalitarianism fell away. There was a hierarchy. The shot-caller had value. And the killer had value. The rest had no voice. Cesar wanted to become the most violent of them all, like everyone else. So for respect he would kill again. And again. And again. In time, he learned another truth: He could also get respect by the method he used to kill. Cesar could kill with the gun. Or he could kill with the machete (a brutality normally reserved for traitors and informants). There was a logic to the macabre choice. To take a man apart with the machete, piece by piece, was to send a message—to his friends as well as his enemies. With the machete, Cesar wielded fear.

Before Mano Dura, the clique was a neighborhood entity. The only homeboys one would know were the other members of his own clique (and rarely did he know anyone at all outside that circle). But prison was a blender. As Cesar and his crew began getting scooped up and shuffled through dozens of jails, they mixed with other members of Barrio 18. Soon they were comparing notes, sharing strategies, and forging alliances: "If you need to kill someone in your neighborhood, call me

60 and I'll send guys who won't be recognized to pull the trigger."
The cliques were still autonomous, loosely affiliated cells. But
they had begun to realize what they shared in common, and
new hierarchies were forming amid the shuffling of ranks in
gang-segregated prisons. In the process, they were becoming
something bigger.

With these new lines of communication, an idea traveled
quickly. The idea that would establish the gangs' stranglehold
over the economy, escalate the war between them, and transform their *raison d'etre* came down as an order from the gangs'
ranks in prison in 2006. Prominent voices in Mara Salvatrucha,
whose new cast of leaders was then coalescing, were also calling
for extortion at a level of something like national policy to support members jailed in the government's ongoing campaign.
At the micro-level of Cesar's block, however, he had first heard
about *la renta* from an American he knew only as "Mr. Lonely."
It was fitting. The Southern California gangbangers had given
them their culture and criminal sophistication, like the baggy
clothes and hand signals they used to communicate. It was the
Americans whose tattoos they had copied and the Americans
again who convinced them to stop making tattoos mandatory—
that's how the police were spotting them. For Cesar, extortion
was the most important idea the Americans brought.

Mr. Lonely came from Los Angeles—came and went, like
a tourist. That's all Cesar knew about Mr. Lonely, except that
he hadn't come to start cliques, only to share information. The
idea he shared that found the most traction was *la renta*. He
described it like this: "Whoever comes to the street pays me,"
Mr. Lonely told Cesar. "I control this table. If someone wants to
sit at the table, they have to pay me." For Salvadoran gangsters,

this was a revelation. They didn't have poppy or coca fields to fight for, as Mexico or Colombia did. Nor had they learned to profit from the transshipment of drugs through their backyard, as U.S.-led interdiction efforts in Mexico and the Caribbean shifted flows to Central America. What they did have was power over their neighbors, the coercive force to tax the sweat of their brows. Cesar realized how much money he was missing out on: He could take a cut of anything that came or went, was bought or sold, in the area he controlled. He could be taxing everything.

Extortion gave the gang a new level of capacity and control. With money, the *palabrero* could buy cell phones so that everyone was in constant communication. If he landed in jail, he could hire a lawyer. With money, Cesar found, he could get away with anything in El Salvador. By the time he became a shot-caller, Cesar had murdered twenty people. In theory the spoils of their violence were supposed to be communal, but accounting was left to the *palabrero*. Gang members didn't receive a salary, relying instead on their leader to take care of their needs, which were often humble, like a place to live if their families kicked them out or money to buy a new pair of shoes. Because police were always confiscating their weapons, a big line item in his budget went to re-arming (most often, with the complicity of the five cops who lived in the area that he controlled and would confiscate guns from other cliques in the zones where they patrolled and sell them back to him in turn, perpetuating a cycle; at other times, he would travel to the "blind spots" along the Guatemalan border, where liberal American gun laws contributed a flow of new weapons to the thriving cross-border contraband trade). Even after accounting for such expenses, however, a

62   margin of opportunity remained. One driver paid Cesar $2,000 a month for the right to deliver beer to the neighborhood, and he could often take in as much as $10,000 each month—enough to embezzle a few thousand for himself.

Just as the drug trade had earlier monetized control of L.A.'s inner-city streets, provoking the bloody gang wars of the 1980s and 1990s, extortion translated Salvadoran territory into wealth, making every block an asset to be acquired. Throughout the years following Mano Dura, the gangs waged vicious turf battles and explosive riots in the overcrowded prisons. A rough benchmark for the viral spread of the strategy can be found in the number of gang-related extortion cases investigated by the attorney general's office in that time, which increased sevenfold between 2003 and 2006. The impact can also be measured in human lives: In 2002, the year before Mano Dura, the annual murder toll was 2,344; by 2006, it had nearly doubled to 4,380, despite the record number of suspected gang members now behind bars.

But Cesar came to see that extortion had another hidden cost. It made the gangs parasites in their communities, exacerbating the cycle of residents informing and his clique murdering informants. This war-making on all fronts—in which each gang was now engaged against the state, its rival, and its neighbors— produced a period of internal consolidation that gave rise to a new leadership.

The waves of violence and repression escalated in the summer of 2010 when a faction of Barrio 18 gave the country a terrifying glimpse of what it had become. The plan, as Cesar understood it, had only been to kill the driver and the fare-collector—a warning to the bus company's owner to pay the extortion demanded for the route. Nothing more. But things got out of hand. On June 20, gang members machine-gunned a bus as it passed through the city center of Mejicanos, then doused it in gasoline and set it on fire. Seventeen passengers burned alive inside. No one seemed to know why it had happened. But it had. And it quickly ushered in a new reality.

The year before, as El Salvador achieved the world's highest murder rate (71 homicides per 100,000 inhabitants), voters desperate for change handed power for the first time to the FMLN, electing Maurico Funes as president. Funes was a journalist and TV personality who had campaigned as a political outsider. But now, confronted with his first political test, he fell back on a familiar formula: a new rash of Mano Dura–style laws backed by a media blitz. By this time, however, the gangs had also learned something about the power of fear and publicity. The day after the new law was passed, the imprisoned leadership of both MS-13 and Barrio 18 sent out word of a nationwide public transport strike, threatening to kill any bus drivers who disobeyed the edict. Over two days, an estimated 60 percent of the country's public transit shut down and the chamber of commerce reported $24 million in lost business. The government, in turn, deployed an additional 2,000 soldiers, along with tanks and heavy machine guns, to reinforce the 3,500 already in the streets. The gangs responded with a call for dialogue. But Funes's new defense minister, David Munguia Payes, who said he had his own plan to reduce the homicide rate, scoffed at the gangs' proposal. "A democratic government like ours," he said, "cannot negotiate with criminal organizations."

The government, Cesar thought, was acting like the gangs had taken aim at the state itself. And the state struck back with

64   a vengeance. Shoot-outs multiplied. The weapons got bigger. Cesar received a phone call from prison with orders to start killing cops because cops were torturing and murdering their homies. Amid the escalating madness, Cesar landed in prison once more. The prospect of serious jail time had a way of clarifying things. Ever since he had killed enough people to call the shots himself, and all the older veterans were dead or in jail, Cesar had been in a position to betray those around him. By now, the leadership knew he had been stealing money and sleeping with other members' girlfriends—an abuse of power for which he might be killed or, at the very least, subjected to repeated brutalities in a prison the gang controlled. When police offered him a chance to become an informant, he accepted.

In exchange for his continued cooperation building a case against his gang, Cesar was freed to fend for himself. He found refuge, ironically, in Mara Salvatrucha territory. Neither his neighbors nor coworkers in the civilian job he landed knew anything about his former ties or the twenty-six lives he had taken. His new life was to be a modest one, lived in constant fear of discovery. One day, he recognized two Barrio 18 members he knew on a public bus. Cesar got off quickly and slipped away. But it was a reminder that in El Salvador no one could hide forever; in time, it's likely he will meet the same end as his victims. And so be it. Cesar's sins, he knew, were his own. The kids he had grown up with had all come from poor, broken families like his, and yet some became doctors and lawyers. Cesar had made his own choices. But still, as he watched the new left-wing government borrow straight from the right's playbook, he recognized something about the role of the

gangs — they made an awfully convenient scapegoat. Who ben-
efits? The drug dealer. The arms trafficker. The oligarch who
cheats the tax system. In a society increasingly beset by secret
iniquities, the gangs were the grimacing public face the rest
could hide behind.

Truce

Like the Los Angeles gang truce two decades earlier, the announcement in March 2012 of a truce between MS-13 and the two factions of Barrio 18 in El Salvador triggered fierce debate. The deal had reportedly been brokered by a government-sponsored mediator, former rebel Raul Mijango, and a Catholic bishop. Under its terms, gang leaders would be transferred to medium-security prisons and allowed to communicate with their associates in order to put an end to the bloodshed on the streets. The truce found support from the Organization of American States, which signed on as an observer to the process, and from some in the NGO community who hoped it could start the gangs down the path to demobilization. Their enthusiasm was seemingly rewarded when, almost as soon as the truce was announced, the murder rate plummeted, cut roughly in half.

The U.S. government and the Catholic church, however, opposed the truce, and mistrust of gang members within the business community scuttled plans for expected development projects in marginalized areas. Sustaining the truce in the face of these pressures required the application of "sticks and carrots" for a complex network of brokers between the imprisoned gang leaders, their lieutenants, and the police. "Discerning what those carrots and sticks were exactly, and who received them, has been difficult," according to a landmark study of MS-13 from the investigative journalism organization InSight Crime. "The Attorney General's office says that as much as $2 million in public funds were diverted illegally to the truce brokers, facilitators, and possibly gang leaders themselves."

When the truce eventually collapsed, the gangs emerged stronger than ever, with a newfound sense of their political power that left "little doubt that the fundamental tipping point in the growth of the gangs in Central America" was "the ill-fated truce between the major gangs in El Salvador," according to a report by Douglas Farah and Kathryn Babineau, *The Evolution of MS 13 in El Salvador and Honduras*. In its wake, leaked videos showed politicians from both parties negotiating with gang members to buy their support for the 2014 elections. A wave of unprecedented violence followed that showcased the gangs' new military capacity as well. The country's security situation "resembles what it did during the 1980s: a low-intensity war," as InSight Crime put it. "The violence is pushing more people to flee to the United States, completing a vicious cycle. Some of these refugees are being recruited into the MS13 in the United States, where they have been tied to another spasm of violence along the East Coast. Some of them are settling in Los Angeles, where the gang is trying to revive cliques to their former glory. Communication, now easier than ever, is increasing among and between cliques. Efforts to supply illicit drugs from the south

68   have picked up as well, while money and weapons are coming from the north to help El Salvador's MS13 fight back against the brutal police-led onslaught."

Carlos knew the names of the men who were coming to kill him. He even knew the name of the gang leader who had given the order. The only thing the informant couldn't tell him was when they would come. His colleagues in the police and army had been getting ambushed around the country or kidnapped while off duty and "disappeared." The attacks would come at night when surveillance was limited and false reports could be called in to stretch their forces thin. So Carlos and his comrades had been waiting for them through the long summer nights, behind sandbag fortifications they built as a frontline defense.

So much had changed since the truce. Carlos had been tipped off to some of the changes that would come when he was still a rookie. In 2011, assigned to a hospital to guard sick prisoners, he had struck up a relationship with an MS *palabrero*, who told him that plans were underway for a gang truce. The gang was going to acquire new weapons and consolidate power, start generating new sources of income, and become a political force. At the time, although the police and gangs might kill each other in a shoot-out, something like a mutual respect still held. But things were about to get ugly. The *palabrero* warned Carlos it was time for a career change.

The next year, the online newspaper *El Faro* broke the story that the leadership of both Mara Salvatrucha and Barrio 18 had been transferred to minimum-security prisons. A gang truce was in the works. Seemingly over one weekend, the gang leaders had brokered a cease-fire that was respected nationwide across the ranks. Over the next month, rival gang members were giving press conferences and issuing joint manifestos together. They had spokesmen and a fancy political discourse, portraying themselves as the people's true representatives, the new guerillas. Almost immediately, the national murder rate was cut in half.

But Carlos wasn't fooled. Sure, the official murder rate had fallen. But the bodies were just finding their ways into clandestine graves. As a show of good faith, the gangs gave up a trove of weapons. But they looked like antiques from the Second World War. By then, he had become an intelligence officer and could see from his newfound vantage that the gangs had begun to acquire advanced weapons. He could also see evidence they were infiltrating the army and police. One soldier had even confided to him that he was a member of Barrio 18. He talked openly about conducting a robbery in uniform while he was supposed to be on guard, and taking three days' leave, armed with his service weapon, to attend a gang party. The other soldiers in the unit confided to him as well. They warned him their comrade was throwing gang signs, threatening to kill them. Carlos quietly reported this up the chain of command and the soldier was removed from his post.

The truce was not without its defenders, especially in the international press. But it did not enjoy widespread popularity among Salvadorans, especially amid reports that gang leaders had been given access to prostitutes and drugs as prison perks. The U.S. vehemently opposed it. And soon others began to see the danger in a negotiation that allowed the gangs to simply kill more people for leverage. As the government began backing away from it, in 2014, the murder rate began to climb once again. In June of that year, Salvador Sanchez Cerén became the first

70   former guerilla to be elected president. He immediately cut off all support for the truce and by year's end had packed the gang leadership back off to maximum-security prisons. One of the most violent periods the country had known since the civil war followed.

The gangs struck like they were mad as hell and twice as lethal. They were organized now, using military tactics, armed with better weapons than the police, including grenades. Carlos had the sense the gangs had asked for some concession that was denied them and, feeling powerful, unleashed their might against the state. Things got ugly quickly. His friends were vanishing one by one. He left for work every day unsure that he would return.

When the attack came, it was more brazen than he expected. On June 22, Carlos and his unit were relaxing after a routine daytime patrol, when two vehicles in the flow of traffic running past their checkpoint drifted to a stop. Suddenly, their occupants popped out and unleashed a storm of automatic gunfire, orange streams blazing from the barrels of their AK-47s and American-made M-16 assault rifles.

The first shot cracked past, just above Carlos's head. He saw fear in the eyes of his sergeant, a hardened veteran, as he yelled, "To the ground!" Carlos dove for cover. Time slowed as his mind raced. Had one of his friends out front already been killed? Were they really being shot at? Or had they only panicked at the sound of a passing truck? He could see clouds of gun smoke hanging in the air, like in a movie, and he smelled cordite. The bullet-riddled sandbags above him were leaking. He knew that they were outgunned, with only one rifle between them. If his enemies pressed their advantage and stormed the outpost, he and his men would be killed. Instead, the gang members fled. Carlos and his colleagues eventually gathered themselves and tried to give chase. But their truck was hobbled by a flat tire.

Daniel slid his cell phone across the table to show me a photo: a manila envelope with two stacks of cash, totaling $10,000 and $25,000. We were seated on the patio of a swanky athletic club in the capital, beside a swimming pool ringed by tropical plants. The intermediary who put us together had warned me that, as a police intelligence agent, Daniel developed more lavish tastes than he had when he was a guerilla. ("It's a fancy place," he said. "He's that kind of guy.") The stack of cash in the photo didn't belong to Daniel, though. It was money from the Ministry of Defense that Daniel said he was ordered to deliver to two MS gang members—a payment that totaled more than half the president's annual salary. Clandestine payments to the gangs ultimately totaled millions of dollars, part of a secret package of concessions to support a truce that would ultimately backfire, transforming the gangs into a military-grade insurgent force and "political extortionists" on the national stage. "The day I quit," Daniel told me, "was when they asked me to deliver this."

Daniel had fought in the civil war. When the new civilian police force was established at war's end in 1993, he considered it a hopeful sign the country was ready to put its divisions behind it. So he stepped forward to serve. But, like Ticas, he soon confronted the PNC's shortcomings, seeing the force as too hastily constructed and serving the whims of politicians. Police had ignored the gangs at their inception, when deportees began taking over public parks in his neighborhood in 1990. Around this time, Daniel became friendly with two of those who would eventually ascend to Mara Salvatrucha's national leadership. But he regarded their rapid rise and the official neglect with alarm; especially when authorities, late to the threat, returned to the old tactics of repression and abuse. This included a tolerance of death squads (like La Sombra Negra), which came creeping back from the corners of recent history, their "social cleansing" campaigns targeting gang members now instead of guerillas. Daniel and some colleagues proposed their own gang prevention strategy, with an emphasis on healthcare and education for at-risk youth, which they tried to pitch to local municipalities. But his superiors weren't interested in prevention, he said, only "beatings and bullets."

Among a generation raised in working-class neighborhoods where these repressive agents became the only familiar face of the state, a new antipathy was born. The gangs expanded quickest in areas where the state was weakest, and by 2000, with the help of dirty municipal-level politicians in both parties, had already made inroads into the lowest branches of the army, police, and local NGOs, according to Daniel. Their influence grew after 2005, when an MS leader named El Camarón began advocating large-scale extortion as a Mano Dura war chest to support the families of the swelling ranks of imprisoned members and fund the purchase of heavier weapons. As the gangs began to administer fiefdoms from within their cages, the government inserted its own intelligence agents, like Daniel, to monitor them, which is how he became privy to the inner workings of the truce. Daniel wouldn't tell me all that he knows, nor how he knows what he could tell me. But what he would tell me, he said, he knows from experience so firsthand that, after resigning his post, it pushed him into hiding for a time, armed with a Glock and a shotgun, in a redoubt he described only as "a very tropical environment."

According to Daniel, the first meetings began in July 2011, in the office of the truce's mastermind, Defense Minister David Munguia Payes. Payes had come up with the idea during the 2009 presidential campaign, when he was part of the security detail protecting FMLN candidate Mauricio Funes. Daniel and others say that Payes saw a deal with the gangs, which would reduce the country's record-breaking murder rate, as the kind of political success that could pave the way to political office. Daniel listed the names of those present, which included, among others, Payes's right-hand man, military intelligence chief Colonel Simon Alberto Molina Montoya, and Raul Mijango, a former guerilla who would serve as an intermediary with the gangs. Only after the initial plans were in place did Payes alert President Funes to what was happening, securing a green light to proceed. Over the next few months, they put the pieces into play.

From the outside, the preparations looked like bureaucratic infighting. (Payes was appointed the Minister of Security, which would give him control over prisons and the police to control negotiations with the gangs, but this was ruled unconstitutional because the peace accords established a firewall between the military and police; instead Payes shuffled personnel to put his people into place overseeing the various branches of the security forces.) They reached out to a military chaplain to help broker the truce and to the prison director to facilitate the transfer of gang leaders into minimum security prisons, where meetings could be arranged. To give the negotiations an air of moral legitimacy, they recruited a few evangelical pastors.

Daniel took out a square blue sheet of notepaper from his wallet and unfolded it on the table. It contained the names of active gang members on the outside that he was tasked with tracking down to ensure that the terms the gang leaders in prison agreed to would be implemented on the street. Still, organization was not the gangs' strong suit. So Payes directed Mijango to help them restructure so that orders from the top could be relayed throughout an integrated chain of command. Daniel borrowed my notebook to sketch out how this worked. The leadership structure he drew resembles a pyramid with three levels above its base: First came the de-facto national leaders in prison, the *ranfla*, who by force of cunning and charisma had established themselves atop the food chain; reporting to them were leaders of the *programa*, each of whom oversaw the shot-callers at the level of the *clica*. For the first time, the territory of the entire country would be divided into zones of control, which would be apportioned in accordance with this hierarchy that connected the foot soldiers to the generals. If before the gangs were like a disorganized crime family of distant cousins, now they resembled something like an army.

Giving taxpayers' money to murderous gangsters was a bridge too far for Daniel. But the money wasn't coming from public coffers alone: Salvadoran narco-traffickers contributed money to pay the gangs as well, he said. Like the Salvadoran government, the narcos also have an interest in minimizing the body count in the countries where they operate, at times, if only because exceedingly high levels of violence draw the Americans' attention and make it harder to do business. A truce would allow them to secure a deal with all warring parties to move their U.S.-bound drugs across El Salvador without interference.

Just as importantly, the rollout of a massive stimulus—in the form of long-awaited jobs and development programs in impoverished barrios that the gangs would demand for their soldiers and supporters—would provide a prime opportunity for money laundering. To this end, the narcos even contributed to help fund the truce. A Salvadoran army officer was dispatched to a meeting with representatives of a Salvadoran cartel to hash out the details. To maintain some semblance of control, under the agreement he secured, the gangs would be paid for guarding drug shipments in cash only, not product. (Paying the gangs in drugs, experience had shown, would only mean a trail of new addicts and, ultimately, more bodies in their own streets.)

Over the course of negotiations, the gangs developed their own agenda. What they demanded of the government was, in part, an alternative that would allow them to come in from the cold: loans to set up legitimate businesses and send some of their members to college. Once again, they wanted social programs and jobs in public works. But now the gangs had learned the value of infiltration.

Daniel thumbed through his cell phone photos until he landed on one of a young man with a square jaw and short-cropped hair squinting at the camera—the military service record of one of thirty-seven gang members inserted into elite branches of the army and police to receive training and intelligence in order to protect the gang. As a result of the negotiations, the gangs would also be tipped off to impending law enforcement raids and granted control of the "blind spots" along the border with Guatemala. Finally, military intelligence facilitated the transfer of previously confiscated weapons to them and, through a Sinaloa intermediary, more advanced arms:

76   Daniel scrolled to a photo of automatic assault rifles, plastic explosives, and detonators.

Rather than a remedy for the structural rot at the heart of the society that had produced the gangs, the truce was a deeply cynical strategy that aimed to serve the interests of these three groups. The FMLN, having accomplished virtually nothing in power, would get a big political win in the face of public anger over epidemic levels of violence. The cartels would get a new money-laundering haven and safe passage for their drugs—from MS-13, Barrio 18, and the government—along a country-wide stretch of the smuggling corridor to the U.S. And the gangs would get money, weapons, and infiltration into the security forces charged with their eradication.

When Cerén took office in 2014 and restarted a war with the gangs, the homicide rate reached an astonishing 104 per 100,000 people—in the capital San Salvador, it was double that—and the country once again was the world's most murderous place. In March 2016, Cerén struck back again with the fist, announcing a campaign of "extraordinary measures." As *El Faro* reported, between January and August of that year, for every cop killed in shoot-outs the police killed fifty-three suspected gang members.

That has backfired, said Daniel. The abuse of gang members alienated those who might have been redeemed by an actual reintegration program, and united all in a new antagonism against the state. In a country of unresolved class tensions that's seen staggering numbers of its people murdered, the fist is deceptively popular, but only perpetuates the conflict. Police lack the capacity to investigate gang violence, and rely instead on a snitch-system that fans paranoia. Civilians get caught in the middle and pay with their lives. The problem has become structural. The government has never had a coherent, long-term strategy for dealing with the gangs, and has done nothing to change the culture that produces them. Even as the gangs grow stronger.

The truce was a crash course in politics. Ever since, any politician who wants to campaign in gang-controlled areas has had to negotiate with the gangs on their terms. Today the gangs have relationships with politicians from both parties, said Daniel, and have financed campaigns in 42 of the country's 262 municipalities, including all of those along the border.

In the last few years, Washington has stepped up its engagement with El Salvador, funneling hundreds of millions of dollars to fight the gangs. But the Americans don't seem interested in watching where that money goes or probing the ties between its allies and the drug-trafficking organizations that have proliferated in the wake of the region's wars.

Daniel warned a CIA colleague that one of his superiors, a member of a specialist group comprising CIA, FBI, DEA agents and their Salvadoran counterparts that meets regularly to coordinate the interdiction of drug-smuggling boats, is also the link between the Salvadoran government and the narcos, and is feeding them misinformation to ensure that only the rivals to favored cartel-affiliates are stopped. But such warnings always seem to fall on deaf ears. Would-be allies among the Salvadoran ranks are now looking to China for more effective leadership in the region. The narcos have been empowered by the sense that the Trump administration couldn't care less about drug-trafficking or corruption, which have become endemic.

After he quit his job as a police intelligence agent, Daniel took a gig as a chief of staff for a mayoral candidate. One day, the candidate received a new BMW as a gift. Daniel showed me one last photo on his cell phone: $1 million in plastic-wrapped U.S. currency that had been stashed inside it.

After all the MS gang leaders were transferred to Ciudad Barrios, a group of businessmen began coming to the prison to meet with them in secret, accompanied by the bishop, said Fausto. Only the gang's top rankings were privy to the negotiations: El Colocho, El Pava, El Diablito of Hollywood, El Crook, El Rata, and Snider. "These were the masterminds," said Fausto. "They determined what information we received and what they wanted to withhold."

Fausto picked up my notebook to draw an outline of their structure, just like the one Daniel had drawn: the national leadership of the *ranfla* at top, then leaders of the *programa*, followed by leaders of the *clica*. Fausto was the leader of a *clica*, responsible for seven neighborhoods. But he was close with Snider, the *ranflero*, who told him things above his pay grade. On the surface, the transaction was morally defensible: the businessmen were helping set the gangs up in legitimate businesses as an alternative to extortion. "They thought that the ends would justify the means," said Fausto. "But among them were always dark thoughts about how to engage in money laundering." In the process, the businessmen taught the gangsters to disguise their revenue streams. And the gangsters played along, pretending to be going legit. Fausto helped Snider prepare one of the investment plans, which they had agreed would be used to launder money from drugs and extortion. But even Snider was tight-lipped about the identities of the businessmen and some of their FMLN allies, telling him, "If you knew about all the corrupt people in the government who are involved in all this, you would be surprised."

Fausto had traveled a long, violent road to end up in the prison where we met. In 2005, only one year after he joined MS-13, he landed a thirty-year prison sentence for aggravated homicide. Following a series of nearly successful escape attempts—one of which involved tunneling out beneath the walls to escape into the jungle—he bounced around between various penitentiaries until 2009, when he landed in the MS stronghold of Ciudad Barrios. For the first time, he saw the scale of what he was part of.

I had last seen Fausto here, in a different prison, a few months before. At the time, his hair was close-cropped and he wore a crisp white shirt with a black scarf draped over his shoulder. He carried a German grammar book and spoke in long, too-deliberate sentences. Fausto struck me as polite but had the air of a man dressed in his Sunday best. A lawyer was working on getting his sentence commuted, and he expected to soon be released. Because Fausto had deactivated from the gang—"crossed the letters," a death sentence if his former associates catch up to him outside—he was planning on leaving the country. But his case had since hit some obstacles, and his release no longer felt like such a sure thing. His hair had grown out, and he had put on weight. A shaft of milky sunlight shone through the window behind him, but Fausto remained in the shadows, his hands folded on the small table between us. His aura had changed. His movements appeared more languid, his smile more cynical. He looked more like a criminal. And sadder.

80   His partner had been receiving death threats since he left the gang, he said. And he was stuck in prison.

     When I asked about Payes, Fausto's demeanor grew serious. "Who else could be capable of getting involved in this type of game?" he asked. It had to be someone with power and a sharp military instinct. In May 2017, El Salvador's attorney general's office issued an indictment against twenty-one former police officers and prison officials—mostly low-level functionaries whose charges were eventually dismissed—who had been associated with the truce. The government's lead witness in the case described how he and other gang members were given fried chicken dinners and flat-screen televisions as incentives to reduce the murder rate. Although the indictment named Payes as the truce's true architect and alleged he was responsible for granting gang members "perks"—including visits from their associates outside prison—the minister of defense was not charged with any crime. According to the *New York Times*, documents detailing Attorney General Douglas Melendez's charges against the conspirators claimed that the truce was part of "a plot that allowed the gangs to reorganize and rearm and 'to make targets of the civilian population, soldiers and the police.'" As Fausto put it, "Salvadorans did not have the balls to touch him, and the authorities did not have the guts to expand the investigation." Of course, this was a moot point since officials from within the Ministry of Justice would always tip them off whenever anyone was coming to snoop around anyway.

     The reality of those perks went beyond televisions and chicken dinners. When a government intermediary first arrived with an entreaty to quell the violence, Fausto said, Mara Salvatrucha's initial demands had been modest: an end to the

invasive strip searches of female visitors by soldiers deployed as
prison guards, which had set off heavy clashes within the prison
walls and against the army on the street; also, access to drugs and
prostitutes. To establish a secure line for negotiations, the military provided gang leaders with specialized communications
equipment that allowed them to talk directly with top FMLN
leaders. Eventually, the military also allowed cell phones to be
smuggled into the prison so that orders could go out to stem the
killing—no small ask, given the legacy of vendettas on the street.
The government began paying both gangs vast sums of money,
Fausto continued, such that MS even began to invest in legitimate businesses abroad to expand its war chest. (This sense of
division between the *ranfla* and leaders outside the prison walls
would deepen as a result of this new wealth being appropriated
from the truce, giving rise to bloodshed within MS.)

As negotiations progressed, the gangs' sense of their own
power grew along with their demands. They asked to be set up
in legitimate businesses, which they could use both to launder
money and to gain a stake in the larger society. In some cases,
MS went so far as to pay for gang members to finish their
schooling. "They were able to place some of them in universities
so they could become attorneys," Fausto said, in the hope they
would "fight to find a better path or a better future within the
government." But their main demand focused on infiltrating the
elite security units that were persecuting them. The gang members tapped for these posts were carefully screened—smart,
clean-cut types with an education.

Mara Salvatrucha's success in lobbying for prison conditions also gave them leverage over the other criminal bands
based there. As a result, the gang was able to consolidate control

82   over all drug-dealing and human-smuggling operations in the streets. For example, MS began to tax coyotes one-third of their earnings (a charge that was eventually passed on to the customers trying to escape the gang's violence). The gang started to see itself as "a Salvadoran mafia," said Fausto. "They began to control every neighborhood, every business, becoming more and more powerful in society."

Fausto told me that what really interested the gangs was the power of the government to work under the table and make certain negotiations with weapons. As a demonstration of good faith, the gangs had made a public show of turning in arms, which was a farce, he said. In his clique, they only turned in old guns that no longer worked, even while the gang was acquiring rocket launchers and claymore mines. During the truce, some gang members from MS-13 and both factions of Barrio 18 were even sent for paramilitary training—in remote mountain areas that had been rebel strongholds during the war. Their FMLN allies sent experienced guerrilla commanders to teach the gang members basic infantry skills, how to stage ambushes, and how to attack police posts. Fausto had told me about this during our previous talk. Still, I found it hard to understand why a government would teach gangs guerrilla tactics that could be used against its own forces. The FMLN had been telling MS that if they "stopped being a gang and instead became a guerrilla, they would receive greater support." Fausto believed this was an attempt to press the gangs into service as shock troops in case the FMLN lost power. (The intermediary who put me in touch with Daniel confirmed that some gang units did receive this paramilitary and political training, which was part of a short-lived plan to transform the gangs into a force that could be used to defend the political gains the party expected to derive from the truce; something like Hugo Chávez's "bloques de apoyo popular" in Venezuela.) Later, when the arrangement with the government began to fray, MS cliques would begin collecting intel on police and military personnel, creating lists of their home addresses, and asking female visitors to memorize the faces of those on guard.

As a result of the power they acquired from the negotiations with the government, the gangs and the narcos eventually reached an agreement in which the gangs would protect drug shipments and the narcos would pay them in money and weapons, Fausto continued. But the greatest corruption comes from the top. "The support that the United States has provided in terms of technology has been very effective. But who has the knowledge or the power at the top to let, say, a boat full of drugs go by? Who diverts the attention of the maritime units?" The oligarchies gave rise to the guerillas, said Fausto, and since the war many of those former rebels have become rich. Now the two groups work together, using the country's common criminals as cover.

"During the truce, there were thousands of disappearances. Why?" Because the gangs never stopped murdering people, but only started disappearing them instead. That duplicity is coming to light in the form of corpses being exhumed from clandestine graves. But the biggest criminals are the rich and powerful, he said, who remain free to hold office, exploiting the people while colluding with those who are the source of their misery.

"It Was Like an Army"

In the wake of the truce, the police once again entered red zones like Manuel's neighborhood shooting first and asking questions under torture, unleashing the worst tactics of the civil war years. On one such occasion, he said, police held him on the floor of an interrogation room and tortured him with electric shocks. Then his interrogators squeezed his fingers with pliers while asking about a list of names of suspected gang members. Manuel was left to languish in an overcrowded cell, where inmates defecated on the floor. They led him outside daily to be subjected to stress positions, naked, and doused with liquid tear gas. He broke down crying. Some of the other inmates were "disappeared" after authorities transferred them to prisons controlled by rivals—a death sentence. When he was finally released, all Manuel could think about was killing the officers who had put him there. In El Salvador, he concluded, human rights don't exist.

His enmity was amplified by the knowledge that some of those abusing him were complicit in the crimes of which they accused him. In the years since Mano Dura, the gangs had grown more powerful along with the ranks of their new allies eager to profit from them. At El Paso, a restaurant outside Santa Ana, Manuel had dined with judges, lawyers, and investigators willing to resolve their criminal cases for a hefty fee. On one occasion, after most of his clique was picked up, the arresting officers told them the names of the gang members who had ratted them out. The clique decided to kill the informants and their families—the police had used them and then released them on the streets to the lions.

But worst of all was the fact that he had left the gang and became *calmado* in 2008. He was embarrassed at the way his son looked at him, always hiding out on the heels of a drug deal gone bad. He made little money. And he was tired of worrying that any moment he could be killed in a shoot-out or murdered by his own gang. One night, he was partying with his friend "El Loco" when he finally broke down. They were surrounded by women, with money and guns on the table. But Manuel felt empty and alone. He picked up his guns—a .38 revolver and a .45 semi-automatic—and said he was leaving. He said he would shoot anyone he encountered on the street and that he hoped it was a cop. El Loco told him he was crazy. When Manuel got home, he called another homeboy and asked him to come pick up the guns—he was done. The voice on the other end of the phone asked him what he would do for a living, but Manuel had no answer. He knelt, put his forehead to his hands, and asked God for a job. A few days later, an intermediary who knew he was looking for a way out found him one—a job program in a new factory that was hiring former gang members ready for a second chance.

86   Which is where I met him—in a factory that produces apparel for the U.S. He credits the program for his ability to leave the gang life behind him. Why aren't there more programs like it, he asked. We were sitting in an office at the factory where he works, which is ringed by an urban fabric of gang-controlled slums. Today kids join gangs because of the money, he said, but 80 percent of them could be convinced to quit if they had a real job. "It's always the stick, the stick, the stick."

Never the carrot. When it introduced the Firm Hand, ARENA promised extensive gang prevention and rehabilitation programs as well. But these were rolled out late, if at all: Mano Amiga (Friendly Hand), a gang prevention program for at-risk youth; and Mano Extendida (Extended Hand), a rehabilitation program that aspired to "teach values, offer spiritual assistance, education, job training, health services, tattoo removal, cultural activities, and sports activities and to facilitate the search for employment." The programs were targeted at the twenty most crime-ridden communities. But the agency tasked with overseeing them was the Secretariat de la Juventud, which was a problematic choice. "During its lifetime," the agency "spent vast amounts of public money on promotion. However, most of its technical staff lacked the necessary expertise and were simply young ARENA supporters who received a generous salary while being groomed as a future party cadre. Overall, the SJ appeared to be a fundamentally weak and politicized institution that was created to demonstrate the Saca government's commitment to prevention and rehabilitation, but displayed neither a vision of comprehensive gang control nor a real interest in it," according to Wolf.

A Salvadoran journalist told me that one of these programs was, in reality, an ARENA intelligence-gathering operation. Gang members would be given jobs, but in order to keep them they would have to give up the names of the leaders of their cliques. This precipitated a period of fierce bloodletting in which those who collaborated were murdered by their gangs. During the truce, he was allowed access to MS gang leaders like "El Diablito of Hollywood," before they were again secluded within the confines of maximum security prisons. "You don't know how many good friends I had to kill because of Mano Amiga," El Diablito reportedly told him. "Friends and family. Dozens."

I asked Manuel if that was true. "That's what I'm telling you. That's what I'm telling you," he said. "They threw this out and said the firm hand against the criminal and the friendly hand goes to the one who wants to work, to—" He paused, trying to remember the word. "—to 'reintegrate' into society. But how are you going to reintegrate into society when you don't have a job, nothing dignified, without any rights?" he asked. "The friendly hand never arrived." In light of the government's failures and the NGOs that make money saying they help ex-gang members—"pure bullshit"—Manuel thinks private industry could launch their own programs.

American policies in the region have long restricted U.S. funding from going to any program where participants had criminal ties—codified into policy in 2012 when the Treasury Department designated MS-13 a transnational criminal organization, alongside Al Qaeda and the Japanese Yakuza. This made it illegal for U.S. funding to go to any organizations engaged with the gang, even jobs programs to help leave the gang life.

But in 2015, as the murder rate surged to 103 homicides for every 100,000 residents—more than twenty times the rate in the United States—the arrival of thousands of unaccompanied

88   minors from Central America at the U.S.-Mexico border caused
the Obama administration to investigate the factors driving
their flight. The results pointed to violence from narcos and
gangs—a study from the Center for Global Development found
that for every ten additional murders in the Northern Triangle
countries, six more children migrated to the United States—
which prompted a reconsideration of the ban and opened the
door to funding some organizations working to rehabilitate
former gang members and give them a way out. In 2017, the
Treasury Department awarded a waiver to the State Department
and USAID to fund the program that rescued Manuel from the
gang. But the waiver must be renewed each year—a relationship
that's tenuous at best under the tenure of President Trump.

In the absence of the carrot, he's seen the stick drive more
than a dozen of his fellow gang members who had been *calmado*
back into the gang life. It's a hard pull to ignore. One of them was
El Mafioso, who as a young man had his mother beg for him to be
released. The other day, Manuel saw him surrounded by about
twenty young lookouts in the process of trying to become active
gang members. "It was like an army," he said.

To understand this cycle of escalation and retaliation and
where it might be headed, I met with Carlos Martinez in the
crowded, buzzing office of *El Faro*, headquarters of the country's hip and scruffy journalistic intelligentsia. Martinez's
family is testament to the paradoxes of El Salvador's histor-
ical elite: His mother is an avowed leftist and devotee of slain
archbishop Óscar Romero, whose assassination marked the
onset of the civil war; her older brother Roberto D'Aubuisson
is the right-wing leader believed to have given the order for

the assassination. Martinez's newspaper produces some of the most consistent journalism about the gang problem in Latin America. He answered my questions in long bursts of targeted oratory, punctuated by cups of water.

In the beginning, he said, the war was between two gangs, a conflict that had carried over from Los Angeles's Macarthur Park to kill untold thousands across Latin America. Extortion monetized the conflict, but it remained a war between two criminal organizations.

The first time the gangs displayed an awareness of their power on the national stage was after Barrio 18 torched the bus full of people. "President Funes created another law, which again prohibited gangs and again gave gang members more years in jail for more things." In response, the gangs launched national strikes that paralyzed the country's public transportation system for days. "That's what the guerilla did during the civil war. The gangs demonstrated this before the truce, 'We can act in coordination and paralyze the public transportation system of this country.' That is a political act," he said. "The truce perfected those possibilities."

The truce exposed a startling degree of sophistication and organizational capacity on the part of the gangs. The politicians had sought them out and dealt with them as equals, and the gangs had learned their political power. Just as significantly, they learned how much they have in common. When the politicians turned on them, the gangs realized they shared more with each other than with the state that persecuted them.

It wasn't until Sanchez Cerén militarized and unleashed the police, Martinez continued, that these two criminal organizations understood themselves to be at war with the state. When

90   Cerén announced that the era of negotiating with gangs was fin-
      ished, new anti-gang units were created and unshackled from
      the traditional oversight of agencies like Internal Affairs. The
      country's vice president announced that police were free to use
      lethal force without fear of suffering any consequences. Things
      got exceedingly ugly. "The police live in the same communities
      that the gang members live in, and the gangs responded sav-
      agely, he said. They killed children in front of their parents. They
      decapitated police in front of their children. They killed mothers
      and they raped wives. And the police responded with the same."
      In the process, "that conflict that had been planted over decades
      in a cycle of revenge, over which so much blood had been spilled,
      that conflict was suddenly redirected toward the state."

      Throughout the history of the gangs, each stage of their
      evolution has been catalyzed by state action. Now the state is in
      a war from which there is no discernible exit. It has managed to
      push these criminal organizations to embrace a political agenda
      while the turf war between them is diminishing toward some-
      thing like a Westphalian peace. "Each gang respects the oppo-
      nent's territory for its criminal activities and what they both
      understand is that the state is their enemy," he said. "What is
      an organization that defines itself by its conflict with another
      gang? It is a gang. What is an organization that defines itself by
      its conflict with the state? I do not know. That is a mutation that
      the state is currently accelerating, and it also asks citizens to
      position themselves in that war."

      To fight that war, they have freed the hand of the security
      forces, he said. When they do that, he continues, "things such
      as the one that I will now tell you about start to happen." Mar-
      tinez recounted the story of a joint patrol of soldiers and police

who entered a community called Zacamil. The gang members, already tipped off by their lookouts, had melted into the neighborhood. Instead, the troops encountered a nineteen-year-old man whose mother had sent him to buy tortillas for lunch. They took off his shirt to search for tattoos, but he was not a gang member. By the time his mother came out to look for him, the security forces were hitting him and stabbing him with a pen to force him to tell them where the rest of the gang members were. When the mother asked them to stop, they pointed their rifles at her and called her an old whore. Finally the neighbors came out and the patrol let him go. "It appears that nothing has happened. It is settled; the boy is free. But a mother witnessed how the state tortured her son, and a son witnessed how the state humiliated his mother." On that day, he said, a mother and a son in a divided society realize they have something in common with the gangs: The state regards them as part of the same class.

This creates a social paradox: The upper and middle classes are the most virulently anti-gang, while the communities in which the gangs have the strongest presence—that is, the people who live directly under their brutal yoke—are the most sympathetic. That's because the gang members, for better or worse, are a part of that community. He told me another story, about the community of Montreal, where the young man who held power was named Oscar. Oscar was smart and ruled with an iron fist. But he also took on a role administering disputes to minimize conflict; which is to say he ruled but also governed. There was a man there who would beat his wife every time he got drunk, which made him the source of a public disturbance. In Montreal, if you call the police, Martinez explained, the gang

92   members kill you because they don't want the police in their neighborhood. So Oscar warned him that if someone calls the police because of him, Oscar would kill him. The man never beat his wife again. Instead, they separated. His wife went to Oscar to say that, despite being grateful that her husband was no longer beating her, he hadn't left any money to support their child. So Oscar told him to deliver a certain sum on a certain day of every month or else he would kill him. "That man is now the most responsible man with his family," Martinez tells me. "This is a true story. I know the man. I know the woman. And I knew Oscar."

For those in the neighborhood, there is no shortage of reasons to hate the gang that extorts their businesses and threatens their guests or worse (if you're a young woman that a gang member takes a fancy to, this is "a curse from which no one can protect you"). Nonetheless, when the police entered Montreal and executed Oscar, the community was indignant. "I was sent a photo of Oscar's corpse. They killed him on his knees. His brain was splattered ahead of his body," said Martinez. The residents in this area might have been grateful to have been liberated from a tyrant, but instead they saw the murder as a betrayal. If the state had hoped to drive a wedge between the gang and the community, it had failed. Of course, this is of little concern to the upper and middle classes, who know the gangs only through the extortion they pay if they own a business or through what they see on television. That is the sector of society that applauded the unconstitutional laws like Mano Dura and all its successors, Martinez said, and continues to endorse, more tacitly, the work of the death squads. As they watch Oscar's corpse on the newscast over lunch, they say, "Excellent! One less gang member."

He continued, "This is the reason why in such communities, where there are a lot of very poor people, the state is not a good school or a good hospital, or a good street, or a good system of public transportation. The state is not good employment. The state is a police officer. The state is a soldier. If the state represented in that police officer or that soldier tortures your son and humiliates your mother, you are generating a division that sums up everything we've been discussing," he said. "What you are creating is a bomb." And if the only indicator you pay attention to is the murder rate, the problem will grow infinitely more complex right under your nose.

At the same time, the gangs are fluid, constantly evolving. So far their biggest mutations have come in response to state action, nearly always the stick. In 2012, at the truce's onset, when he asked the MS leadership if they were going to disband as part of the truce, Martinez said, "They almost ate me alive." In the last interview he did with their representatives, one year ago, they told him they were open to dismantling the gang if the government would negotiate with them in public with an organization like the UN as witness, and if the government would propose a reintegration and rehabilitation law to consider reviewing unjust sentences. "These are not stupid conditions. The evolution of gangs, I think, will depend on the stimuli and the possibilities they receive. If they receive, I think, more and better stimuli from drug trafficking than from the state, I think it is likely to evolve in that direction. If they receive stimuli in another direction, it is very likely that the gang will end, although it seems absurd at the moment, sitting at a negotiating table discussing its own disbanding."

Ministry of Defense

At lunchtime, Carlos Rivas took a break from our interview to file his paperwork to run for president. It was the deadline to do so and he'd been leaning toward the decision throughout two days of talking, interrupted by a steady stream of calls from the circle that the retired colonel cultivated over three decades of military service. Rivas's career reflects a commitment to the military he served being held to its highest standards: taking custody of a notorious right-wing death squad commander who he turned over to authorities; giving critical information to a U.S. congressman investigating the government's role in the murder of six Jesuit priests, which proved a turning point for U.S. support of the right-wing government that Rivas served; advocating an end to the amnesty law that shielded his country's war criminals. Already his resume had nearly cost Rivas his life: He had survived two assassination attempts. In light of all this, the decision to run was no small matter, coming over the objections of his family who

worried he was less likely to win office than to be murdered by
his rivals. The colonel's political connections, they feared, had
already cost the family so much.

As is often the case in El Salvador, his story begins in the
civil war—or the earliest days of what would become the war,
at least, when he saved the life of Sanchez Cerén, who, in 2014,
would be elected the country's president. In 1978, Cerén, still a
budding insurgent, was arrested for subversive activities. Rivas
was then a captain in the army. But the two had been friends
in grade school. At the time, Rivas recalled, "Those who were
lucky were released and those who weren't, well . . ." So Cerén's
mother called Rivas's mother, who called her son. Rivas petitioned all the relevant authorities on Cerén's behalf, but to no
avail. Finally, he made his appeal to the president himself, who
ordered Cerén's release.

A decade later, in the final years of the war, Rivas's mother
died. Cerén, who had risen to become a commanding general
of the FMLN, came across her obituary in the newspaper, and
passed along his condolences to Rivas through an intermediary. The following year, presumably seeking to repay an old
favor, Cerén sent a warning to Rivas not to venture out into
public places during the first two weeks of November. Rivas told
only his family (and President Cristiani, who did not believe
him). On November 11, 1989, for the first time in the war, thousands of *guerilleros* came storming out of the mountains into
government-held cities, precipitating fierce urban warfare and
a campaign of aerial bombardment that would make the offen-
sive the deadliest confrontation of the decade-long conflict,
claiming 17 percent of the war's total casualties. The scale of

96   the losses would convince both sides that, without an infusion
      of more foreign military support, neither would be able to van-
      quish the other.

      Arguably more significant in hastening the war's demise,
      however, was a particular act of violence that took place against
      the backdrop of this larger carnage. On November 16, a unit
      of the U.S.-created Atlacatl Battalion stormed a university
      campus and executed six Jesuit priests, their housekeeper, and
      her teenage daughter. (Right-wing forces considered the Jesuits
      to be "the brains of the guerilla" for their embrace of Libera-
      tion Theology and outspoken stance on social justice.) In the
      investigation into the attack, considered a tipping point for U.S.
      involvement in the war, Rivas gave critical evidence to U.S. con-
      gressman Jim McGovern that implicated those in the highest
      reaches of the Salvadoran military.

      Rivas retired in 1991. The next year, at the signing of the
      Chapultepec peace accords that ended the war, he reached out
      to Cerén, who thanked his old school chum for having saved
      his life. They celebrated that Christmas Eve together in Cerén's
      home, then New Year's Eve at Rivas's. For a while they kept up a
      cordial friendship. But their paths diverged again as Cerén began
      his career in politics, and Rivas settled into private industry,
      starting his own security company.

      Throughout, Rivas stayed close to the generations of offi-
      cers he had groomed in his years as an instructor at the military
      academy, remaining something of a military busybody. Although
      he knew about skeletons still hidden in the closets of powerful
      men, Rivas made no secret of his concerns over reintroducing
      into the new army and police those involved in massacres,
      assassinations, kidnapping-for-ransom, and drug-trafficking

over the course of twelve long years of conflict—the reason, he suspects, that he was targeted in two assassination attempts in the late 1990s, by men he believes were police agents.

In March 2014, after Rivas had aired these views again in an extensive interview with the news site Contrapunto, Rivas's youngest son, Guillermo, came to him in alarm. There was talk in military circles of repealing the amnesty laws, and a Spanish court was moving ahead with its own trial for the murders of the Jesuits (five of whom were Spanish citizens). People were talking, Guillermo told his father, saying that any one of their family might be killed in reprisal for the things that Rivas had said. "I told him not to worry," Rivas recalled. Guillermo fired back that his father never listened, pushing Rivas to set a meeting with his old friend Sanchez Cerén, the president-elect. "I told him I would do it once he became president," he said. But by that time, it was too late. "To my surprise, they did kill my son."

Early on the morning of April 23, Guillermo dropped off his wife and young daughter at a relative's house and returned to his home in a suburb of the capital. Upon entering the house, forensics would show, he was surprised by a gunman who stalked him from room to room, firing a total of seven rounds into his body. Before he expired, Guillermo was able to shoot back, emptying the revolver he carried into his assailant and killing him in the exchange.

The chain of events that followed next stands out from the average murder investigation in El Salvador in many ways. Within minutes, officials from several agencies had arrived at the crime scene, and a ready-made story—that the killer was a disgruntled former employee at Rivas's security agency— was being peddled to the press. Also unusual was the presence

98   of three senior security officials, including Lieutenant Oscar
Gomez, a member of an army intelligence unit who, according
to the police report, beat homicide investigators and the med-
ical examiner to the scene, arriving on the heels of the first
responders and insisting on seeing the gunman's body.

When Carlos Rivas arrived, about an hour later, the gunman's body was still in the house while his son's corpse lay
in a police pickup truck. The forensics team had yet to arrive.
Gomez greeted him by name and rank, and announced that he
was from military intelligence and had been sent to help investigate the murder. Police would not let Rivas inside to see the
assailant, who, it was already being posted on social media,
was supposedly his former employee. One of the investigators
agreed to take a photo of the man's face. Rivas didn't recognize
him. He called his office to confirm that no one had been fired
in the last year. The killer's body bore no trace of identification,
except for a two-dollar bill folded into a triangle, which, Rivas
learned, was the calling card of an assassin. He was later identified as Felix Vladimir Romero Morales, a gang hit man.

That night, David Munguia Payes called Rivas to express
his condolences. The defense minister said he would be at
the funeral the next day. The two had last met in 2009. Rivas
had made a habit of meeting with each new defense minister.
He would offer his opinions, get a sense of their agenda, then
keep an open line. But their conversation had been short. Rivas
offered his assessment that the greatest security threat facing
the country was drug trafficking; Payes told him not to worry
about the narcos; the gangs were the real problem. Rivas countered that the two were related, but the new defense minister expressed no interest in that assessment, and the two

had parted ways. Munguia Payes had no recollection of such a meeting taking place.

The retired colonel greeted the defense minister the next day at his son's funeral and introduced him around. Then the two stepped outside to talk on the patio. Payes told him to look to his own business to find the culprit behind Guillermo's death. Rivas objected, having already looked into that theory and found it to be untrue. But the younger man was insistent. As Rivas recalls, he had had enough, blurting out that he recognized a cover-up and suspected his son's death had been a military operation. (Munguia Payes recalled this conversation differently, saying that Rivas merely thanked him for attending.)

Over the next two weeks, Rivas called Lt. Gomez to try to get an update on his son's case. Finally, Gomez agreed to meet him. But on the day they were supposed to meet, Gomez went missing. A few days later, he turned up dead.

Rivas undertook his own investigation. He spoke to the hit man's mother, who described a red car—the same color and make as Lt. Gomez's—that came to pick up her son the week before the shooting that left both their children dead. Rivas also spoke to a friend of Lt. Gomez, who told him Gomez had said he'd been threatened by a superior for signing his name on the crime scene report. Gomez had been worried he would be killed to wrap up loose ends. (The death certificate listed the cause of death as a buildup of liquid and blood in the lungs; his boss would go on to claim that Gomez had been drunk and gotten beaten up by gang members.)

Eventually, Rivas took his dead son's advice and wrote to the president. When he didn't hear back, he wrote again without answer. Finally, he went public with it. The fourteen-page letter

100 (which he copied several members of the U.S. Congress on) detailed the state of threat under which he and some members of the press who reported on his story had been living. As an example, he cited a July 27 incident in which the police found a man surveilling Rivas, armed with a Glock pistol and an AK-47, who reportedly told police he was part of an intelligence unit and that he was tasked with following Rivas and his friends.

Rivas laid out the circumstances of his son's murder and why he believed it was plotted by defense officials. In no uncertain terms, the letter spelled out how, since the truce, Munguia Payes had converted a military intelligence unit into a death squad tied to gang hit men. Officials were involved in the planning and execution of the murder, hiring a Barrio 18 hit man, Rivas wrote. He mentioned three names involved in the plot: Munguia Payes, his adviser Colonel Simon Molina Montoya, and Jose Luis Merino, a senior FMLN leader. Rivas warned that El Salvador is in the depths of an "institutional, political, economic, social, moral, and military crisis" owing to corruption, impunity, and organized crime.

In response, Molina threatened to sue for defamation. A spokesman for El Salvador's attorney general, however, told the *Christian Science Monitor* there was no evidence that a conflict at the family business had anything to do with the murder and that investigators were still waiting on the military to provide information on the case.

Rather than the success story the U.S.-brokered peace process was billed as when international organizations packed up and pulled out of the country, Rivas says, the reality was the beginning of a dark new era in El Salvador. Twelve years of war had corrupted combatants from both sides. Yet many of those who had turned to kidnapping or the drug trade during the conflict—whether to fund their side's war chest or their own—were absorbed into the new security forces as a result of the peace accords, paving the way for alliances with organized crime. The U.S. has worked with corrupt officials from both parties ever since. It's a message that Rivas has tried to relay to his American allies. "The reality is, since the peace accords, all the governments—all the governments, those from the right as much as from the left—have been deceiving you," he told me. "All are connected with the narcos."

Rivas later put me in touch with a friend of Lt. Gomez's, whom I'll call Francisco. He and Gomez had been close in their years at the military academy together, and Francisco had later served alongside American troops in Iraq, before resettling in the United States. Francisco and Gomez had reconnected. Gomez wanted to know more about seeking refuge in the U.S., Francisco told me, because he felt his life was under threat.

Worried he was a loose end about to be tied up, Gomez confided in his old friend about the mess he was in. According to this account, Lt. Gomez had been recruited to oversee the operation to kill Guillermo Rivas. The plan was to use a professional gang hit man who would stage the murder to look like a robbery-gone-bad. When Francisco asked why Gomez would accept such an assignment, he said he had been passed over for promotion and would soon be forced into retirement. The officer who recruited him said that if Gomez completed the mission, they would find a way to get him promoted to captain.

When Gomez transferred into the military intelligence unit, Francisco told me, he learned about the operations that had been carried out to buy the support of gang leaders for the truce: cell phones smuggled into the prisons, money exchanged, weapons transferred. Some in the police force had opposed negotiating with gangs, however. In the end, they discovered the gangs were deceiving them. They hadn't stopped killing, but only started hiding their victims. And they were only being empowered by the ability to summon a police chief to complain about the rate of police raids in a particular zone.

After Gomez met with the hit man, he was given a vehicle to surveil the target and exfiltrate the killer on the day of the shooting. But in the course of his surveillance, Gomez failed to spot the small revolver Guillermo Rivas carried. And the whole operation turned with its cylinder: In his last moments, when Rivas squeezed off the volley of shots that tore through his attacker, he had set off a chain of events that Gomez had feared would claim his own life, too. Rather than escape, a would-be robber at large, the hit man lay dying. The first responders arrived within minutes—a foot patrol had been in the neighborhood when the shots were fired—and although Gomez got there soon after, the house had already been cordoned off. He called his boss to report that one of the men inside was believed to be alive, and he feared it was their hit man. The officer reportedly replied that if the *sicario* made it to the hospital alive it could mean trouble. He was a liability and could implicate them all. What Gomez did next, he did in panic, identifying himself to Colonel Rivas and signing the police report. His boss was furious and had threatened him. Gomez knew he was now the last witness who could implicate the rest—a liability. Francisco asked why he couldn't tell his story to someone higher up the chain of command for help. Gomez told him there was no one to turn to: When he met the minister of defense, his superior had introduced Gomez as "the guy who is going to take care of the job for us." Four days after Francisco last spoke to him, Gomez was dead.

A few days after my talk with Rivas, a bipartisan group from the U.S. Congress issued a letter urging the Trump administration to consider targeted sanctions against Jose Luis Merino and five other officials implicated in organized crime around Central America. (Notably, Merino, a senior FMLN official and deputy minister of foreign affairs, was the only one on the list who holds office, which grants him immunity from prosecution in El Salvador.) The letter invoked the Magnitsky Act, whose primary author, Congressman Jim McGovern, is an old El Salvador hand who worked with Rivas on the investigation into the murder of the Jesuit priests. "I thought that he was truthful," he said of Rivas's character, when I reached McGovern by phone. "And I thought that he cared deeply about the future of El Salvador."

In present El Salvador, McGovern sees a culture of impunity fostered in the Cold War hysteria of the past, when the U.S. government was so focused on its enemies that it ignored the most shocking crimes of its allies—even when, as in the case of his own investigation, the evidence implicated those in the highest reaches of power. "Reagan bought into this domino effect that somehow El Salvador was going to become a communist country. I remember, in '88, just being startled at how the embassy and our government just routinely turned a blind eye to some of the most horrific atrocities imaginable. And confronted with overwhelming evidence, they still kind of went along to get along . . . and as a result we have a situation today where impunity is still a problem, where corruption is still a problem. Extrajudicial killings are still a problem. The human rights situation is horrible," he says. "It's maddening that my government, the United States government, continues to be clueless in how our policies have made things worse, not better."

The country's trajectory has been dispiriting. The truth commission at war's end was "an important statement," he said, but lacked teeth. The 1993 passage of an amnesty law effectively guaranteed that war criminals from both sides would never face justice. Rather than galvanizing the international community for "a mini Marshall Plan" to rebuild the country, as the U.S. should have, "we cut economic aid significantly and we walked away. After we spent billions of dollars destroying the country." McGovern greeted the FMLN's win in 2009 with some optimism, expecting the party would clean up the corruption that had thrived under ARENA rule. But instead, "a big chunk of the FMLN bought into the corruption."

Rather than a success story, today he cites the U.S.-backed peace process in El Salvador as an example of how *not* to end a war. And in reality the war never quite ended. "During the war I felt safer than I do now when I walk in the street in El Salvador. There's more violence happening today, there's more people losing their lives each day today than there were during the war. And you had 80,000 people perish over the decade-long war." As a result, people are again fleeing the country in record numbers because they fear for their lives. "When you think about the current status of things, it goes directly back to our involvement. I mean, we helped screw that place up. And we have a moral obligation to be more constructive and more helpful in helping them resolve some of these challenges. But

it doesn't seem that Congress is up to that task, nor is the
administration."

To the extent that policymakers think about El Salvador at
all, McGovern said, they ignore the causal factors driving the
country's violence. "Instead, all we do is we bitch about Salvadoran migrants and talk about how everyone who wants to
come here is a bad player. These women and children are fleeing
horrific violence. And the violence that they're fleeing is fueled
by our terrible policies over these years. And unless we decide
to take a different look at things there, you're going to have
more and more migrants coming to the United States."

Right now, McGovern is still trying to push the Salvadoran
government to hold accountable the members of a U.S.-created
battalion that massacred hundreds of civilians at El Mozote in
1981, which he hopes might at least send a signal that could help
deter abuses going forward. Even in this, he told me, Payes is the
chief obstacle. The attorney general is onboard, but "the bottom
line is the minister of defense. He's providing absolutely zero
cooperation. I mean none." McGovern has a request pending
with the Trump administration to exert some diplomatic pressure, but "the Trump administration couldn't give two shits
about human rights."

And what do U.S. intelligence agencies know about the bad
actors they partner with?

"We know a hell of a lot more than we let on," McGovern
said. "I mean, we're not stupid." The problem, he has come to
believe, is that too many in government think their job is not to
make waves. "They're just kind of looking the other way, hoping
that the pot doesn't boil over," he said. "Well, it's boiling over."
Some argue that if they push the Salvadoran government too

hard then they won't be helpful on drug interdiction or immigration. "There are a million excuses. But the bottom line is, I think the U.S. government knows a lot. And I think we knew a lot back in the '80s. And they just put up with it and explained it away and rationalized it. I think the same thing in the present day. Which is one of the reasons we're part of the problem now."

When Rivas finally got a sit-down with Sanchez Cerén, "he told me he had read my letter and asked what I needed from him," Rivas said. In response, Rivas asked Cerén to support the attorney general, who was pursuing a case against the truce's functionaries—for "illicit association" with the gang members they arranged prison transfers for—in order to pressure them to name who had been giving the orders. "But then nothing happened."

It reminded him of a story from the final days before the civil war, when Rivas was part of a four-man military commission that looked into the working conditions of peasants cultivating coffee on the country's plantations. He and the other officers reached a conclusion that, without some basic land reforms, pervasive inequality in society was going to provoke an insurgency. The president himself agreed and, looking to save his government, brokered an agreement with the plantation owners to give up some land to the workers. They struck the deal on a Saturday and drank together in celebration. On Monday, word came back that the oligarchs had changed their minds and wouldn't comply with any of the terms to which they had agreed. Seizing on the rift, Roberto D'Aubuisson began to conspire to create a new right-wing party, which set the stage for the coup and tipped the country to war. In the forty years since, Rivas has become ever more cynical about the structure of power in El Salvador: The system works for those it works for. "They don't change anything," he said, "because they don't want to."

Tracking down General David Munguia Payes proved difficult, especially after June 2019, when he was replaced by incoming president Nayib Bukele. Munguia Payes seemed to have been avoiding the spotlight in the months since and sounded understandably shaken when he answered my call and learned that I was an American reporter with questions about the truce. Some of my sources had made allegations against him, I said, and I wanted to give him a chance to respond. He was out of the country at the moment, he told me, but asked that I call back in a week. Late the following week, after a few more delays, we got on the phone. We agreed to go down the list, one allegation at a time.

I began by asking for his response to the accusations that Rivas had made so publicly.

"We in the armed forces had no motive to assassinate the son of Colonel Rivas," Munguia Payes told me. First, he said, because they don't do such things. Second, because he wouldn't have recognized Rivas if he had run into him on the street. The military intelligence officer who had appeared at the scene within minutes of Guillermo Rivas's murder, Munguia Payes continued, had been investigating the killing of another serviceman nearby, which had occurred two weeks before, when a (mistaken) report came in that the Rivas shooting involved a military officer—that was why Gomez had responded in the first place. The initial investigation had concluded that Guillermo Rivas had been killed "possibly because of problems he had with other people," said Munguia Payes, or else because his assailant (the gang hit man) was there to rob him, but Guillermo pulled a gun. What motive would the military have to kill Rivas's son, he asked. Murdering innocents was a dark chapter of the wartime past.

I recounted what Rivas told me: his sources in Sanchez Cerén's inner circle alleged that Cerén had been considering him to replace Munguia Payes as defense minister when he took office.

"That's not true," Munguia Payes responded. "At no moment did President Sanchez Cerén think about Colonel Rivas. President Sanchez Cerén called me, and he asked me if I would accept the position of minister [of defense]. And in the end, I accepted it." Rivas may have had that expectation because they were friends at school or something, he said. But it didn't make sense. Anyway, logic dictates that the target in that case would have been the colonel himself, not his son.

(For his part, Rivas argues that, given his connections in Washington, D.C., his own murder would have drawn too much scrutiny; killing his son and spreading the rumor it was a gang-affiliated murder, however, would have tarnished his family's reputation and eliminated him as a rival.)

"The truth is that I truly believe, due to desperation, Colonel Rivas has lost his head a little bit," Munguia Payes said. "I believe that the death of his son, which I lament very much, has affected him. Not only emotionally, but also in his head."

We moved on to the truce.

When I asked about the origins of the truce, he talked for about five minutes: the idea had come from a think tank; one of the first things they did was get the Organization of American States to sign on as an observer; he and President Funes had each traveled to the U.S., pitching the plan to American officials—John Kerry's State Department, the FBI, the World Bank. "It was a public policy of our government to resolve, or try to resolve, the problem of violence in the country," he told me.

I asked if it was true that the first meetings to implement the truce had taken place in his office in July 2011. He paused for a long moment. He truly couldn't recall, he said.

Was it true that he had directed Raul Mijango to help restructure the gangs organizationally so the truce could be implemented more effectively?

"No, no, no. It's not true. I never spoke with Mijango about that. Yes, we were interested in their communication with the people outside, that they ordered them to stop killing," he said. But he would have had no authority to order Mijango to do anything anyway, since he was not his subordinate.

Multiple sources had told me that payments were made to gang members to buy their support for the plan.

"Totally false," he replied. "Totally false." That was just an idea that people had talked about in the media because they couldn't understand how the epidemic levels of violence had dropped off so quickly. "But never was a cent given to anyone." To begin with, he said, he didn't have any such money to have paid anyone. Then, he seemed to qualify his earlier statement (after all, his FMLN colleague, Security Minister Benito Lara, had been seen in videos offering gang members millions of dollars in microcredit right after the truce fell apart). "Besides, as I understood it, they didn't give money to anyone at this time." In the trials that had gone forward against lower-level participants in the truce, he continued, no one talked about having received money during this time.

I said that I had heard that military intelligence had helped bring phones and comms equipment into the prisons—"totally false," he said. If "other political actors" did this in other time periods, he couldn't say, but he had no knowledge of it.

What about the transfer of weapons to the gangs? No, he said. Nothing like that has come to light. And what would have been the source of the weapons and the money, he asked. Where would those have come from?

I had wanted to come back to that point about the money, I told him. I mentioned two names: one belonging to a Salvadoran army officer; the other, an alleged boss in the Perrones cartel to whom this officer had been dispatched, I was told, in order to negotiate some of the terms of the truce.

"No, no, no. That's totally false. I don't even know that man," he said. "We never had contact with the Perrones." If they had, he told me, the Organization of American States would have detected it and denounced them immediately. "This is the first time I hear anyone mention contact with the Perrones."

For clarification, I asked Munguia Payes which of the two names he didn't recognize. He was referring to the alleged cartel boss, he said. Yes, he knew the army officer. But the officer hadn't been involved in anything like the situation I had described. "It seems to me totally obscene and ridiculous," he told me.

Payes said that he couldn't assure me that the cartels or other criminal actors had no intentions of instrumentalizing the truce. But if they did, he never found out about it. And he remains convinced that nothing like that ever happened in the end.

I asked whether the gangs had been granted control of the blind spots along the border as part of a deal with the Salvadoran drug traffickers. "I don't know that," he said. "All of this

seems to be out of line and ridiculous." As far as he knows, he
said, no cartel was ever involved in this process.

When I asked if gang members had been given paramilitary training so they could serve as shock troops, as in Venezuela, Payes informed me that we would have to be wrapping up the interview soon. He then went on to deny the allegation.

Had the Salvadoran government been providing bad intel to American agencies to protect drug traffickers? "Totally false," he said. To the contrary, under his watch they stopped tons of drugs at sea and were one of the most effective countries in this respect.

I asked how it could be the case that I was hearing such consistent allegations from people who hadn't met one another—from both a police intelligence agent and a gang member, no less? And that others had heard this from their own gang sources too. How could there be such consistency between their stories and yet he, as minister of defense, had never heard any of this?

This was his first time hearing about any of this, he said, and in any case the information I had been given was totally false. His conclusion was that people must be making up stories. Then he thanked me and hung up.

After our conversation, I reached out to Douglas Farah. He had been the United Press International bureau chief in El Salvador during the civil war and, afterward, the *Washington Post's* bureau chief for Central America. Today, he is a national security consultant and, as a senior fellow at the National Defense University, had published a report that suggested we had covered similar ground in El Salvador.

After *El Faro* first broke the story that a truce was underway, Farah told me, he had interviewed Munguia Payes on national television. The government was still trying to pretend that it hadn't been directly involved in the truce negotiations. Munguia Payes, he said, "was absolutely unable to explain how all these agreements had been reached without the government having negotiated with the gangs." In the years since, Farah's reporting with gang sources helped fill in the story of what had happened.

I asked what his investigations had revealed about the involvement of Salvadoran narco-traffickers in the truce. (There are two major narco-traffickers in El Salvador—the Perrones cartel and the Texis cartel—and, according to a 2012 report from the United Nations Office on Drugs and Crime, both are able to operate effectively due to the protection they have received from the Salvadoran state.) One of Farah's sources, he told me, was the emissary who was taking written proposals between Munguia Payes and the Texis cartel. "So we know with a high level of certainty that the cartel de Texis negotiations were specific, relating to specific routes and specific front companies that were going to be set up and specific concessions that would be granted."

He disputed Munguia Payes's claims about the truce on several points. "I would say that there is a clear record of those negotiations leading to gang members receiving military training, the gang members receiving weapons—particularly hand grenades—from the military. And the ability of the gang members to begin to act with absolute impunity if they played within the rules outlined by the minister of defense. And the ministry of defense clearly played a direct role in articulating and executing the truce with the understanding that it was going to benefit both the administration of Funes and, I would say, certain drug cartels that could have a free run through the northern corridor of the country," he told me. "That's without a doubt."

Triangle of Power

On a beautiful Saturday morning, I met Dagoberto Gutierrez on the campus of San Salvador's Lutheran University, where he teaches political science and serves as vice rector. During the civil war, Gutierrez was a member of the guerillas' high command. Afterward he held an FMLN seat in the legislature, but had since grown disenchanted with the rule of his former comrades. We sat to talk in his spartan office, which is decorated with images of Che Guevara, Lenin, and Marx. I'd come to hear what he thinks about the role of El Salvador's legacy of class conflict in the new war raging in the streets. And what to make of the gangs who have adopted the tactics of his own insurgency—torching buses, ambushing police, melting into the countryside—and claimed to be its inheritors. Gutierrez walked me through a Marxist reading of Salvadoran history with the air of someone who was tired of the particular story he has to tell, but still finds an acerbic joy in its telling.

"We've had six wars in our history," he said. "The first one, the most disgraceful, was in 1524 when the damned Spanish

114   invaded us and did a great deal of damage." Three centuries
later, the descendants of those invaders—the newly inde-
pendent country's ruling elite—looked to international markets to develop El Salvador's nascent economy. They focused
exclusively on indigo, leaving the indigenous masses and the
peasant farmers to concentrate on the land where indigo did
not grow. Then, in the mid-nineteenth century, chemical dyes
were invented and the market for indigo plummeted. The landowning elite replaced indigo with coffee, which grew just fine in
the zones occupied by the country's poor. A massive land redis-
tribution followed that left the vast majority of the population
landless and the owners of the new coffee plantations rich. This
was the birth of the Salvadoran oligarchy. "Here the owners are
members of the same oligarchy that in 1864 began accumulating
capital, destroying the communal land," he said. Those land-
owners ruled with a feudal authority that only grew over time,
securing a series of constitutional amendments that granted
ever more power to the fourteen landowning families that have
dominated El Salvador's economic life ever since. These were
the conditions that produced the civil war, he said, and its end
did nothing to resolve the underlying inequalities that had given
rise to it.

The state of war today is a direct result of the conditions
negotiated to end the last war, he continued, which simply created a new ruling class—an alliance between part of the guerillas and part of the oligarchy. Under Washington's guidance,
this new elite oversaw a period of economic reform that trans-
formed the country's class map, allowing the rich to shore up
new gains. "A neoliberalism was applied that was brutal. Total.
Orthodox. Blind. Absolute. That privatized everything," he

says. The fortunes of the farmer and the worker were allowed to wither. "The industrial plant was disassembled and it was said that El Salvador would be a service economy. Nothing like this happened, nothing like this happened."

He continued, "Here, in my country, the king and the queen is the market. Everything is business. Everything is bought and everything is sold. And everything has a price. Even human beings." Today, five blocs dominate the political landscape. "The first bloc is that of the gangs. They have a lot of economic and financial power," he said. "The gangsters are capitalists. The second bloc is that of the guerilla. Strong capitalists and pensioners. The third bloc is that of the drug traffickers. Very powerful. All the oligarchy takes part in the drug trafficking. The gringos know it very well, but their hands are tied. Washington cannot act. The fourth bloc is that of the traditional landowner oligarchy," he continued. "And the fifth bloc is that of the oligarchic financial bourgeoisie. These five blocs do business among themselves. They all know each other. And no one is more powerful than the other. There is no dominant bloc in this moment." As a result, the political system, whose allegiance is divided among these groups, is shaky and uncertain. But it is the gangs who are on the rise. "The gang is a political and military power. Total control over the territory of the entire country. They control all the communities, all the neighborhoods, and negotiate with all the political parties."

Negotiation with the gangs is a fact of life in El Salvador, he said. In most communities, the gang is the sovereign and people must make their daily accommodations with that authority or they will be killed. Businesses negotiate in order to enter a gang's territory or else their trucks are robbed and their

116   employees murdered. Both political parties negotiate in order to run campaigns. This is reality. But good negotiation requires strength. The gangs are wily and have learned to take advantage at every crossroads, while the Salvadoran state is weak. In the case of the truce, the government chose as their goal an indicator—the murder rate—that the gangs could manipulate by putting more or fewer bodies in the street, as they saw fit. This was foolish. "Now the government is determined to annihilate the gang with blood and fire. And it is failing," Gutierrez said. "Because every political phenomenon needs a political solution. The military way works, but only when it is perfectly managed, with fine military coups. But a bloodbath without limits does not work. The government is being defeated. And the gang is on the rise militarily, with military coups that are every time more sophisticated."

What the situation calls for, Gutierrez believes, is a combination of repressive and political approaches working in tandem. But the Salvadoran state has been eviscerated, said the old Marxist. And American support is no substitute. "Washington has intellectual problems," he told me, "because they don't understand, in the first place, that this is a war." It is not a "violence problem" or a "crime problem," but a war that's been running for thirty years. It has become structural and demands a long-term strategy—a war that cannot be fought with soldiers and helicopters alone.

I asked Gutierrez what this portends for the future. His answer was bleak.

"The phenomenon that is coming is called Somalization," he said. "It is a phenomenon that, sociologically, began to register many years ago. Today it is appearing in the cities. Whole neighborhoods are enclosed and shuttered with gates and bars. Somalization is defined by the fragmentation of power. Without the state," he said, almost hissing with contempt. He picked up a pen and a sheaf of white papers. "And there's an agonizing government, without prestige and without authority. So Somalization is the process that advances." He began writing. On each page, he scribbled TORTILLAS, without explanation. He continued. "It is not a good panorama."

"The oligarchs are not concerned because it is still not their turn. But it will come. The oligarchs make their enemies the same as them. That's what they did with the guerilla." He paused but did not look up from his task. "Washington is living the worst chapter of its history," he said. "It's an empire that has lost its hegemony. And, as all empires, it does not realize it has lost it, or does not want to accept it. And that means they won't be able to understand what is happening in small countries like mine—so small that it has no value. And this is very dangerous."

Although today the gangs comprise members of all the classes, he continued, most are still marginalized young people. But now they are to be found in the universities as well. The gangs are training their future lawyers and doctors, economists and military intelligence officers. A new class consciousness is being born under the noses of the old guard. "The oligarchy doesn't realize that power is running out of their hands," he said. "That another oligarchy is forming in the hands of the gang."

"I'm a veteran of the drug war. I was a cop for almost thirty years in this county," said Al Valdez, seated out back of a Mexican restaurant near his former Anaheim precinct. Valdez is tall, with thinning black hair swept back over his head and a cop's penchant for profanity. In the 1980s and 1990s, when Southern California was a gangland killing field, Valdez worked under-cover narcotics, then ran gang homicide investigation units for two decades. He would go out on a call on Thursday night and work straight through the weekend, moving from murder scene to murder scene. In that time he helped draft some of Califor-nia's gang enhancement laws in response to the violence. But all that did was overcrowd prisons—"the new Jim Crow system," as he sees it now—until the governor was forced to open the gates and free thousands of convicts. In the classes he teaches on transnational gangs at UC Irvine, Valdez admits that America failed to solve its own gang problem, just like the war on drugs. "I'm embarrassed to tell my students that my very first felony arrest as a cop, in 1979, was a man in his thirties who had a joint," he said. "And he bought three years in state prison for it. For half a joint."

Experience has made him skeptical about the country's ability to tackle complex, interrelated problems like its drug habit, the gangs it exported, or the tide of emigration from the Central American countries where those gangs are now entrenched. "The U.S. treats symptoms, not causes," he said. "Americans live in an instant society, and that's the Achilles' heel of our government. We need instant results and num-bers. And you can't measure what you prevent." As a result, U.S. policy in Central America has long favored the fist, despite widespread consensus that the militarized, mass-incarceration approach has only exacerbated the conflict.

Valdez first went to El Salvador with the Washington Office on Latin America, a human rights research NGO, to evaluate the country's gang prevention programs—"a frickin' joke"—and

encountered corpses in the street of young men with the Spanish
word for "trash" carved into their bellies. "Who did it? Nobody
knows. You talk to the eyewitnesses and they tell you behind
closed doors, when you promise not to tell anybody, that they
saw a police car pick them up. But officially the *comandante*
would tell you, 'My guys aren't involved.'"

Instead of eliminating the gang problem, Valdez told me,
the death squads are driving emigration among a whole new
segment of the population, the gangs' support base. Every
month or so, Valdez interviews newly arrived immigrants.
"The people from Central America tell me that they're afraid
and one of the reasons they're moving is the suppression program that's ongoing. They go after Gang Member A, and if they
can't find Gang Member A they find Gang Member A's brothers
and sisters. And if they can't find Gang Member A's brothers
and sisters, the family disappears. And that's what's fueling the
migration north." In 2018, Attorney General Jeff Sessions issued
a precedent decision that removed both gang and domestic violence as grounds for asylum. "He tactfully told the world that
we're sorry that you're victims of domestic violence and gang
violence. It's not the U.S.'s responsibility to protect you in your
country. It's your country's responsibility." What that misses,
he said, is that the Salvadoran government itself is the agent
persecuting its people. "And it's so corrupt in some areas that
the country, the military, and the police are actually doing a
form of genocide to the citizens, camouflaged as a cleanup."

He continued, "What the current administration doesn't
understand is the reason people are leaving their country." Over
the years, Valdez has interviewed thousands of undocumented
immigrants, and the two primary reasons they come to the U.S.

120   are poverty and violence. "Putting people in jail and building walls is not going to solve that." Rather than spending billions on security cooperation with Mexico and Central American countries, he said, the U.S. would be better off investing more through the United States Agency for International Development to foster businesses and jobs programs in Latin America.

Instead, in June, President Trump suspended U.S. aid—totaling hundreds of millions of dollars—to El Salvador, Guatemala, and Honduras for failing to stop the flow of migrants. He threatened to seal the border and slap Mexico with tariffs if officials don't do more to stop the movement of people and drugs across the border. U.S. border and development officials warned that could imperil recent gains in El Salvador, and in the long run would only mean more migrants showing up at America's doorstep.

In the absence of more concerted economic development programs, the security side of the equation will likewise continue to be shaped by American demand for illegal drugs—estimated at more than $100 billion per year, according to Rand Corp. "We are a consumption country," said Valdez. "We have less than 5 percent of the world's population. As a nation, we consume over half of the world's illegal drugs."

Central America has the unfortunate circumstance of being located between the world's biggest cocaine producers—Bolivia, Colombia, and Peru—and the world's largest consumer, the United States. Through the 1980s, the main trafficking route between them ran across the Caribbean on Florida-bound smuggling boats. But ramped-up U.S. interdiction efforts there eventually made the land route through Central America a better option, a development solidified by the 2008 Merida Initiative

in which the U.S. traded increased military and economic support for an escalation of Mexico's war against the drug traffickers. This has pushed the cartels deeper into the Northern
Triangle and into closer relationships with the *maras*. The
result has made gang membership appear to be the only viable
path to any kind of material progress for countless young men,
and contributed to El Salvador, Honduras, and Guatemala's
frequent standing among the most violent and crime-ridden
countries on the planet.

"We know that the Mexican cartels have infiltrated Central American countries. The Zetas and Sinaloa cartels are down
there," Valdez said. "It's the drug business! Northern Triangle
countries have become transshipment countries. What the
gangs are now doing is they're acting as muscle for the cartels.
They get paid in money and product."

I asked about the truce and what I had heard about it being
used to launder money and secure a transit route for U.S.-
bound drugs.

"A safe transit route," he interjected, correcting me. "If you
have the right process in play, your drugs can travel with help
from the police because they know they're expecting a yellow
van. And then you get your 150 kilos, 200 kilos, 300 kilos
across." A moment later, he continued, "That's exactly what I
heard." Valdez characterized his sources as "gang members and
citizens in El Salvador."

The gang members Valdez talked to had genuinely hoped the
truce would help them "to no longer be societal lepers in their
country," he said. After Cerén took office, "he declared a suppression program that's turned into a de facto war down there,
where it's the government against the gangs." Valdez recently

122   advised a doctoral student who spent two years researching the geography of murders in El Salvador. Along the way she secured access to the government, the military, and police. In the end, she was surprised to find her data revealed patterns of systemic collusion between the gangs and all three branches. "She was very upset. She was crying at the time," he said. "The politically correct thing to say for the government is, 'We don't work with the gangs and we're against them.' But what the head says is not always true of what the hand does down there."

As a result, the gangs are "getting smart," adapting to benefit from corruption and diversifying their operations. "In Honduras, MS tries to cooperate with the police," he said. "And Eighteenth fights them." Mara Salvatrucha is also assuming control over the tourist industry there. "They're becoming globalized. Truly globalized. And we've failed to recognize this."

At first the gangs were a surrogate family. Then, with extortion, they became a business. Today they are a sociological phenomenon and also a force capable of corrupting or challenging a state. Feeding off the cross-border flow of drugs and guns and people, the gangs have merged with currents of illicit supply and demand that shape reality across borders, binding countries rich and poor, and are mutating toward some new form of international crime that won't easily be walled off and confined behind national boundaries.

Valdez believes that the gangs' international alliances, enabled by corruption across Latin America and the spread of cheap cell phone technology, is creating a triangle of power that connects the East and West Coasts of the United States and Central America. In the early 2000s, law enforcement began to see signs that East Coast cliques of Mara Salvatrucha were developing

vertical leadership structures. First in Fairfax County, Virginia.
Then in New York, Georgia, and South Carolina. By 2008, it had
reached the West Coast. Valdez compared it to the process that
created the Italian Mafia. "It came from the gangs of New York,"
he said. The ethnic makeup of the city's dominant gangs had
changed with each new group of immigrants streaming in. After
an influx of Italian immigrants, a similar restructuring gave rise
to the Gambino family and La Cosa Nostra. Valdez sees evidence
of a similar internationalization taking place that may give rise
to "a Brown Mafia." The FBI has intercepted conference calls, he
said, with gang leaders from all three regions on the line.

Epilogue

That his government would cut a deal with such people was the most devastating blow to morale a cop could imagine. "The government in my country is garbage," said Carlos, seated at the kitchen table of a modest apartment in New York City, where the U.S. government had recently granted him asylum. It was three years since Mara Salvatrucha had ambushed his police checkpoint, sending him and his men diving for cover. But their fear had only grown with the gangs' strength since. "The gangs are never going to disappear," he said. "Never." Now they have become the springboard to power for whichever politician offers them the best deal, dictating which candidates those who live under their yoke must vote for—on pain of death.

When I pressed for details about the circumstances that had preceded that June 2015 ambush, Carlos told me to turn off my audio recorder. What I can say about the story that followed is that it centered on an extrajudicial killing, then a betrayal of his elite anti-gang unit by a member of Mara Salvatrucha who had infiltrated it. And so the cycle continued. Today the Salvadoran government values the rights of a gang member more than the rights of a citizen, he went on, and the life of a gang member over that of a cop. More than a dozen of his friends have died at the hands of the gangs—the last one just a year earlier. Israel Ticas dug his dismembered corpse out of a hole. As the body count piled up, many in the ranks became convinced that something had to be done.

"A death squad is something that nobody knows about," Carlos said, his voice dropping to nearly a whisper. "It's something with no identity. Very delicate." His boss told Carlos he had met with his own superiors and they had been given instructions. "He said the orders to create the death squads came from the top," Carlos told me. Carlos counted himself lucky to have been a member of a police unit in which the rest shared his conviction and call to serve. But, even among them, few knew about the death squad. They were a tribe within the tribe.

When I asked how the squad operated, he described it as a beautiful thing. Unlike policing, he was given all the resources and support that he needed to get the job done. His day job gave him ample opportunity to surveil the gang members who would be their next targets. He had a gift for listening as if he weren't listening closely and got the best intel hanging around murder scenes, staying quiet, soaking up everything. The victims' families were always so raw that they spoke without a filter, naming names without any thought about the consequences. And he would be there, mentally recording the names of suspects. Then, under the guise of an investigation, he would show up at the gang member's house to take photographs and make a report, doing the work of a police officer. He would return later with his accomplices to do the work of the death squad.

The first person he murdered this way had been part of the assault team that carried out the attack against him. When the moment came to execute him, Carlos got a call from his superior warning that a police patrol was in the area. The death squad members were all wearing their police uniforms and couldn't afford to be caught by their colleagues. So he was instructed to kill with a knife. *A knife? Damn.* He let out a hiss, recoiling at the memory. *Well, he is just a gang member,* he told himself. Even after Carlos had slit the man's throat, his victim was gurgling at him, trying to curse. Carlos landed a swift knee to his head, knocking him to the floor.

Their second target was easier. They took him into the hills and dug a ditch. Then Carlos shot him in the head and let him fall into it. For good measure, Carlos smashed his skull with a large rock. He showed me a photo on his cell phone in which he was dressed in his police uniform, carrying a rifle with a cord wrapped several times around the butt—a cord he used to strangle five people. Of the thirty-five murders his squad was responsible for, Carlos took part in thirteen of them. For each of those murders, he returned to the scene as an investigating officer.

Perhaps inevitably, Carlos's work caught up with him, and the gang began to target him and threaten his family. Gathering documentation from his colleagues to corroborate the threats, he set out to make the journey north, traveling overland through Guatemala and Mexico to the U.S., where he petitioned for asylum. Because the threats against him had continued even after he had quit his job, Carlos's lawyer was able to win him asylum on the grounds that he'd been persecuted as a member of a "social group" (i.e., "former police officers"). He was not alone in doing so. In March, the *Washington Post* identified fifteen

former Salvadoran police officers in the process of being reset-
tled as refugees by the UN, and six in the U.S. Their war against
the gangs had been lost.

As we talked in his cramped New York City apartment,
looking back on his career and what had become of his country,
Carlos detailed a litany of macabre scenes in which he had taken
part. He was clearly traumatized and still processing. After a
few minutes, he cut himself off.

"But I liked it," he said of the death squad. Carlos remained
confident in the righteousness of their cause. "I endorse it as a
Salvadoran citizen," he told me. "We did good work."

I would like to thank the whole CGR team for their support: Nicholas Lemann, Jimmy So, Camille McDuffie, Miranda Sita, and Lee Levine. Special thanks to my reporting partner, Juan Carlos, without whom I would have struggled to apprehend so much of what I found.

T. W. Ward, *Gangsters Without Borders: An Ethnography of a Salvadoran Street Gang*, Oxford University Press, 2012.

Maras: Gang Violence and Security in Central America, edited by Thomas Bruneau, Lucía Dammert, and Elizabeth Skinner, University of Texas Press, 2011.

Mark Danner, *The Massacre at El Mozote*, Vintage, 1994.

Erik Ching, *Stories of Civil War in El Salvador: A Battle over Memory*, The University of North Carolina Press, 2016.

Sonja Wolf, *Mano Dura: The Politics of Gang Control in El Salvador*, University of Texas Press, 2017.

Ioan Grillo, *Gangster Warlords: Drug Dollars, Killing Fields, and the New Politics of Latin America*, Bloomsbury Press, 2016.

Juan José Martínez D'Aubuisson, *A Year Inside MS-13: See, Hear, and Shut up*, OR Books, 2019.

InSight Crime, *MS13 in the Americas: How the World's Most Notorious Gang Defies Logic, Resists Destruction*.

NOTES

INTRODUCTION

18   ranks consistently among
the world's most violent nations:
"Homicide Monitor," Igarapé
Institute and the United Nations
Office on Drugs and Crime, https://
homicide.igarape.org.br.

24   "break into our country":
"President Donald J. Trump's State
of the Union Address," January 30,
2018, https://www.whitehouse.gov
/briefings-statements/president
-donald-j-trumps-state-union
-address/.

25   Americanized gangsters
produced a sociological
phenomenon: Wolf, "Street Gangs of
El Salvador," p. 43.

25   mass deportations changed
everything in the country: Sonja
Wolf, "Street Gangs of El Salvador,"
in *Maras: Gang Violence and Security
in Central America*, edited by Thomas
Bruneau, Lucía Dammert, and
Elizabeth Skinner. University of
Texas Press, Kindle Edition.

26   "iron fist" measures to much
fanfare: Wolf, "Street Gangs of El
Salvador," p. 62.

26   populist means to attract
voter support: "Mano Dura was a
punitive, populist move designed
to enhance the electoral appeal of
ARENA rather than to mitigate the
gang problem." Sonja Wolf, *Mano
Dura: The Politics of Gang Control in
El Salvador*, University of Texas

Press, Kindle Edition, p. 4. See also
Wolf, "Street Gangs of El Salvador,"
p. 59.

26   gangs' power has only grown
as a result: "Though popular, these
policies in most cases failed to
reduce crime and may have indirectly
led to a growth in gang membership.
Mass incarcerations increased the
burden on already overcrowded
prisons, many of which are
effectively run by gangs. There, they
recruited thousands of new members
and expanded their extortion
rackets." Amelia Cheatham, "Central
America's Turbulent Northern
Triangle, Council on Foreign
Relations," October 1, 2019.

27   transit corridor for an
estimated 88 percent of U.S.-
bound cocaine: Wolf, "Street Gangs
of El Salvador," p. 56.

CHAPTER ONE

29   Alex Sanchez: Author interview
with Alex Sanchez.

30   a declassified 1982 State
Department memo: Joan Didion,
Salvador, Vintage, 1994.

31   infamous U.S.-created
battalion: Mark Danner, *The
Massacre at El Mozote*, Vintage, 1994.

31   spending more than $4.5
billion: Cara E. McKinney, "Twelve
Years a Terror: U.S. Impact in the
12-Year Civil War in El Salvador,"
International ResearchScape Journal,
2015, Vol. 2, Article 5.

134   31   **Joan Didion observed:** Joan Didion, *Salvador*, p. 66.

31   **roughly a million of them left:** Al Valdez, "The Origins of Southern California Latino Gangs," in *Maras: Gang Violence and Security in Central America.*

32   **"a large scale exodus of undocumented Salvadorans":** "Text of President Ronald Reagan's letter to Salvadorean president Jos Duarte regarding the new U.S. immigration reform and control act for El Salvador," Declassified Documents Online, Document ID Number: 2004090102848, accessed on http://www.history-lab.org.

32   **writes Al Valdez:** Al Valdez, "The Origins of Southern California Latino Gangs," p. 25.

34   **anthropologist T. W. Ward:** T. M. Ward, *Gangsters Without Borders: An Ethnography of a Salvadoran Street Gang*, Oxford University Press, 2012.

36   **50,000 members in 450 gangs:** Al Valdez, "The Origins of Southern California Latino Gangs," p. 26.

37   **gang defectors later described:** Valdez, p. 26.

37   **"at least a degree of discipline at the street level":** Valdez, p. 41.

38   **Angel de la Muerte:** Author interview with "Angel de la Muerte," former member of MS-13. Also: interview with Alex Sanchez.

40   **"fodder for the flourishing prison industrial complex":** Elana Zilberg, "Refugee Gang Youth: Zero Tolerance and the Security State in Contemporary US–Salvadoran Relations," in *Youth, Globalization and the Law*, ed. Sudhir Alladi Venkatesh and Ronald Kassimir, Stanford University Press, 2007, p. 65.

41   **estimates by sociologist Douglas Massey:** "Chain Reaction: The Causes and Consequences of America's War on Immigrants," Douglas S. Massey, Julian Simon Lecture, presented at the IZA Annual Migration Meeting, May 2011, Washington, D.C.

42   **"claim and achieve record deportations of criminal aliens":** "The Disastrous, Forgotten 1996 Law That Created Today's Immigration Problem," Dara Lind, Vox, April 28, 2016.

44   **Manuel:** The story comes from the author's interview with "Manuel," a pseudonym for a former MS-13 member.

47   **Manuel wore a police uniform:** "There are documented cases of the police renting out their uniforms, guns, and badges to the gang so MS 13 could carry out kidnapping and assassinations with impunity." Douglas Farah and Kathryn Babineau, "The Evolution of MS 13 in El Salvador and Honduras," *Prism* 7, No. 1, p. 70. The author also heard this firsthand from a source in Honduras who had recently been loaned police uniforms and a police vehicle for a hit.

47   **fosters a cooperative and codependent military and**

criminal regime: Enrique Desmond Arias, "State Power and Central American Maras: A Cross-national Comparison," in *Maras: Gang Violence and Security in Central America*, p. 123. See also Sonja Wolf, "Street Gangs of El Salvador," p. 52.

47 MS-13 thrived not despite, but because of, the state: See also: Chapter Two, interview with Cesar; Chapter Three, interview with Carlos, Daniel, and Fausto; Chapter Four, interview with Carlos Martinez; Chapter Five, interview with Carlos Rivas; Epilogue, interview with Carlos.

CHAPTER TWO

48 U.S. set to work building up a new civilian police force, the PNC: "U.S. SECURITY (Senate— March 05, 1992)." Fas.org. p. S2874. Retrieved October 16, 2017. Mary Katayanagi, Human rights functions of United Nations peacekeeping operations, p. 77, "Policia Nacional Civil." PNC. Retrieved October 10, 2018.

49 in the form of death squads: James Bargent, "Has Gang Violence in El Salvador Sparked a Death Squad Revival?" InSight Crime, May 23, 2014. See also: "Presciently, a United Nations investigation conducted in the early 1990s warned that the old right-wing death squads of the civil war period had metamorphosed into organized crime networks but could be reactivated to commit politically motivated assassinations," Wolf, "Street Gangs of El Salvador," p. 52. See also: Joint Group for the

Investigation of Politically Motivated Illegal Armed Groups, *Report of the Joint Group for the Investigation of Politically Motivated Illegal Armed Groups in El Salvador* (San Salvador, El Salvador: 28 July 1994), transmitted with letter dated 11 August 1994 from the UN Secretary-General addressed to the President of the UN Security Council (S/1994/989).

49 "a generation of adolescents": Carlos Martinez, "Who Taught the MS13 Politics?" InSight Crime, January 3, 2019.

50 strong correlation between U.S. deportations and homicide rates: "El Salvador's Politics of Perpetual Violence," International Crisis Group, Report No. 64, December 19, 2017.

51 "All the world blamed Francisco Flores": Author interview with Carlos Martinez.

52 "transnationalization": Zilberg, "Refugee Gang Youth."

52 "Rudolph Giuliani": Michael Lohmuller, "Giuliani's 'Broken Windows' Won't Fix Central America," InSight Crime, March 18, 2015.

53 "Mano Dura was not a plan": Author interview with Rodrigo Avila.

54 19,275 gang-related detentions: FESPAD, Estado de la seguridad pública y la justicia penal en El Salvador, 2004 (San Salvador, El Salvador: FESPAD Ediciones, 2005), 13. See also: Wolf, "Street Gangs of El Salvador," p. 59.

136

56 **"a market where everything is bought and sold":** Roberto Valencia, "How El Salvador Handed Its Prisons to the Mara Street Gangs," InSight Crime, September 3, 2014.

57 **Cesar:** Author interview with "Cesar," a pseudonym for a former Barrio 18 member.

60 *la renta*: See also: "Killers on a Shoestring: Inside the Gangs of El Salvador," by Óscar Martínez, Efren Lemus, Carlos Martínez, and Deborah Sontag, *New York Times*, Nov. 20, 2016. See also: "5 Ways the MS13 Launders Money," Felipe Puerta, InSight Crime, Sept. 7, 2018.

62 **In 2002, the year before Mano Dura, the annual murder toll was 2,344; by 2006, it had nearly doubled to 4,380:** Carlos Martínez, "Who Taught the MS13 Politics?" InSight Crime, January 3, 2019.

63 **threatening to kill any bus drivers:** Martínez, "Who Taught the MS13 Politics?"

63 **"cannot negotiate with criminal organizations":** Martínez, "Who Taught the MS13 Politics?"

CHAPTER THREE

66 **a truce between MS-13 and the two factions of Barrio 18:** The story of the truce is told in InSight Crime's report *MS13 in the Americas: How the World's Most Notorious Gang* Defies Logic, Resists Destruction, p. 19.

67 **"Discerning what those carrots and sticks were exactly":** *MS13 in the Americas*, p. 20.

67 **"the ill-fated truce between the major gangs in El Salvador":** Farah and Babineau, p. 68.

68 **Carlos:** Author interview with "Carlos," a pseudonym for a former police intelligence officer.

68 *"El Faro* **broke the story":** Óscar Martínez, Carlos Martínez, Sergio Arauz and Efren Lemus, "Government Negotiates Reduction in Homicides with Gangs," *El Faro*, March 14, 2012.

71 **Daniel:** Author interview with "Daniel," a pseudonym for a former police intelligence officer.

71 **Clandestine payments to the gangs ultimately totaled millions of dollars:** Farah and Babineau, p. 61.

72 **tolerance of death squads:** See also: Bargent, "Has Gang Violence in El Salvador Sparked a Death Squad Revival?"

72 **"social cleansing" campaigns:** See also: Wolf, "Street Gangs of El Salvador," p. 52.

74 **Salvadoran narco-traffickers contributed money to pay the gangs as well, he said. Like the Salvadoran government, the narcos also have an interest in minimizing the body count:** Farah and Babineau, p. 61.

76 **for every cop killed in shoot-outs the police killed fifty-three suspected gang members:** Azam Ahmed, "'They Will Have to Answer to Us,'" *New York Times Magazine*, November 29, 2017.

77   **link between the Salvadoran government and the narcos:** "The CIA-Contra-Crack Cocaine Controversy: A Review Of The Justice Department's Investigations And Prosecutions," USDOJ/OIG Special Report, December, 1997.

78   **Fausto:** Author interview with "Fausto," a pseudonym for a former MS-13 member.

80   **an indictment against twenty-one former police officers and prison officials:** The indictment: Fiscalía General de la República, DENUNCIA DE ANTEJUICIO, Ref. Fiscal: 28-UFEAD-SS-2016 and Ref. 20-UFEADH-2016. See also Ahmed, "'They Will Have to Answer to Us,'" and Nelson Rauda Zablah, "Fiscalía captura a los obreros de la Tregua," *El Faro*, May 4, 2016.

80   **the indictment named Payes as the truce's true architect:** Carlos Martinez and Nelson Rauda Zablah, "Fiscalía había elaborado un borrador para pedir antejuicio contra Munguía Payés," *El Faro*, May 19, 2016.

80   **the minister of defense was not charged with any crime:** Leonardo Goi, "El Salvador Defense Minister Played Key Role in Gang Truce: AG," InSight Crime, May 18, 2017. See also: Efren Lemus, "Juez exonera a obreros de la Tregua y pregunta por qué Fiscalía no acusó a Munguía Payés," *El Faro*, August 30, 2017.

80   **"a plot that allowed the gangs to reorganize":** Alberto Arce, "El Salvador Throws Out Gang Truce and Officials Who Put It in Place," *New York Times*, May 21, 2016.

81   **The gang members tapped for these posts were carefully screened—smart, clean-cut types with an education:** "MS-13's recent success is derived in part from a strategy, begun at least four years ago, of infiltrating members into the police and military, and sending selected cadres to universities to become lawyers, accountants, and MBAs," Farah and Babineau, p. 60.

CHAPTER FOUR

84   **the police once again entered red zones:** Author interview with "Manuel."

86   **a factory that produces apparel for the U.S.:** Danielle Mackey and Cora Currier, "El Salvador Is Trying to Stop Gang Violence. But the Trump Administration Keeps Pushing Failed 'Iron Fist' Policing," *The Intercept*, October 2, 2018.

87   **designated MS-13 a transnational criminal organization:** "Treasury Sanctions Latin American Criminal Organization," U.S. Department of the Treasury Press Center, Oct. 11, 2012.

88   **every ten additional murders in the Northern Triangle countries, six more children migrated to the United States:** Michael Clemens, "Violence, Development, and

138   Migration Waves: Evidence from Central American Child Migrant Apprehensions," Center for Global Development, Working Paper 459, July 27, 2017.

89   **"The truce perfected those possibilities":** Author interview with Carlos Martinez, July 25, 2018.

91   **Zacamil:** Cora Currier, Natalie Keyssar, "El Salvador's Youth Are Trapped Between Gang Violence And Police Abuse," *The Intercept*, Jan. 12, 2018.

CHAPTER FIVE

94   **Carlos Rivas:** Author interview with Carlos Rivas in San Salvador, July 27 and 29, 2018.

97   **extensive interview with the news site Contrapunto:** Alberto Barrera, "El Coronel Si Tiene Que Decir," *Contrapunto*, March 1, 2014.

97   **forensics would show:** Hector Silva, "Murder of Colonel's Son Raises Questions Over Role of El Salvador's Military," InSight Crime, September 9, 2014.

97   **firing a total of seven rounds:** Seth Robbins, "El Salvador murder pits retired colonel against ghosts of the civil-war era," *Christian Science Monitor*, December 9, 2014.

97   **officials from several agencies had arrived at the crime scene:** Seth Robbins, "El Salvador murder pits

retired colonel against ghosts of the civil-war era."

99   **Rivas undertook his own investigation:** Hector Silva, "Murder of Colonel's Son Raises Questions Over Role of El Salvador's Military."

99   **The fourteen-page letter:** Author obtained the letter from Rivas.

100   **A spokesman for El Salvador's attorney general:** Hector Silva, "Murder of Colonel's Son Raises Questions Over Role of El Salvador's Military."

103   **a bipartisan group from the U.S. Congress issued a letter:** "Bipartisan Group in Congress Urges Trump Administration to Utilize Global Magnitsky Sanctions in Central America," U.S. House of Representatives Committee on Foreign Affairs, August 2, 2018.

104   **"a big chunk of the FMLN bought into the corruption":** Author interview with U.S. congressman Jim McGovern.

112   **the Perrones cartel:** *Transnational Organized Crime in Central America and the Caribbean: A Threat Assessment*, United Nations Office on Drugs and Crime, September 2012.

CHAPTER SIX

113   **Dagoberto Gutierrez:** Author interview with Dagoberto Gutierrez.

117   "I'm a veteran of the drug war": Author interview with Al Valdez.

119   death squads are driving emigration: Bryan Avelar and Juan Martínez D'Aubuisson, "El Salvador Police Using WhatsApp, Facebook to Run Death Squads," InSight Crime, August 24, 2017.

119   In 2018, Attorney General Jeff Sessions: Katie Benner and Caitlin Dickerson, "Sessions Says Domestic and Gang Violence Are Not Grounds for Asylum," New York Times, June 11, 2018.

120   in June, President Trump suspended U.S. aid: Lesley Wroughton and Patricia Zengerle, "As promised, Trump slashes aid to Central America over migrants," Reuters, June, 17, 2019.

120   American demand for illegal drugs—estimated at more than $100 billion per year: Beau Kilmer, Susan S. Sohler Everingham, Jonathan P. Caulkins, Gregory Midgette, Rosalie Liccardo Pacula, Peter Reuter, Rachel M. Burns, Bing Han, Russell Lundberg, "How Big Is the U.S. Market for Illegal Drugs?" RAND Corporation, RB-9770-ONDCP, 2014.

121   "We know that the Mexican cartels have infiltrated Central American countries": See also "The CIA-Contra-Crack Cocaine Controversy: A Review Of The Justice Department's Investigations And Prosecutions," and Wolf, "Street Gangs of El Salvador," p. 56.

EPILOGUE

124   "The government in my country is garbage": Author interview with "Carlos."

126   The death squad members were all wearing their police uniforms: "The death squad members—dressed in police and military uniforms—entered their targets' homes under the guise of executing fake search warrants and either executed their victims on the spot or took them to other locations to be killed." Parkey Asmann, "Police Again at Center of Latest Death Squad Uncovered in El Salvador," InSight Crime, October 4, 2019.

Columbia Global Reports is a publishing imprint from Columbia University that commissions authors to do original on-site reporting around the globe on a wide range of issues. The resulting novella-length books offer new ways to look at and understand the world that can be read in a few hours. Most readers are curious and busy. Our books are for them.